OBTAINING YOUR
FINANCIAL BLACK BELT

Power and Control Over Money

Les Traband

Duncan Nelson, Copy Editor - Professor of English,
University of Massachusetts at Boston
1999

Copyright © 2000 by Lester J. Traband

ISBN 0-7414-0223-8

Published by:

Buy Books on the web.com
862 West Lancaster Avenue
Bryn Mawr, PA 19010-3222
Info@buybooksontheweb.com
www.buybooksontheweb.com
Toll-free (877) BUY BOOK

Printed in the United States of America
Printed on Recycled Paper
Published January-2000

Contents

Foreword

As a woman who has been in the public eye for many years, I know how powerful American culture is in having people think that they absolutely must have more – more money, more time, more things, more everything. The constant bombardment of messages from the media, advertising and entertainment industries of which I have been a part for many years has seeped into every corner of people's lives and has colored their experience of themselves. Although we all know at some level that we are whole and complete people, the messages of the day tell us that we must be

Younger
Thinner
Taller
Smarter
Richer

Or someone more than we are now to be ok.

This constant quest for more has most people running in endless directions pursuing the possession of things that make no real difference to their lives.

In his book, Les Traband begins to reveal what is at the heart of this obsessive behavior that traps us all. Les speaks potently and clearly about the condition of scarcity in which we live. He tells us through stories; stories about himself, his wife and family and about many people and circumstances that reveal the ways that we are trapped in the vicious cycle of scarcity.

Fortunately, Les does not leave us there. He gives us the tools, the distinctions, the inspiration and the examples to transform that condition of our lives to the context of sufficiency where

There is enough
We have enough
And most importantly –
We are enough

I am grateful to Les and to all of the people with whom I have worked in The Hunger Project for inspiring and empowering me to see the wholeness, the integrity, the fullness and sufficiency in my own life and in the lives of others.

The Hunger Project, where Les and I became friends, gives a context of responsibility and sufficiency that engenders new distinctions for living and being that enable us all to know deeply and profoundly who we are and that we are sufficient. In that moment of recognition of our own "enoughness" we are complete, we are fulfilled and we experience our own integrity and the integrity of the world around us. I am grateful to Les for this wonderful book and for the way he and his wife, Lee, have lived their lives. They have done it openly and you will see through reading these pages that they hide nothing. From their lives and from this book, we can learn a great deal.

-Valerie Harper
Star of stage and screen

Preface

This book is my way of sharing with you my breakthroughs in relating to money. In my work in both the insurance field and charitable fundraising I have seen much suffering in regard to money. I now know from having experienced this suffering myself that it isn't necessary.

With this book, and all of the other work that I do, I intend to have us all be free from the hold money has on us so we can use it to express ourselves, our commitments and out intentions to make things happen.

My commitment is to have this world work for everyone in every way. One way that it doesn't work is that, according to United Nations statistics, over one billion (20%) of the people on earth are malnourished, which means they go to bed hungry every night and the little they eat doesn't provide the energy and stamina needed for them to make a contribution to society. Even those of us who have enough to eat, adequate shelter, clothing, and a few luxuries are thwarted in our desire to contribute to the world by an unhealthy relationship with money.

Most of the people who will read this book are in this category; i.e., lead a life of comfort and quality. But there's something missing from their lives that no one talks about or even suggests is missing.

WE LIVE AS IF THINGS ARE SCARCE.

I participate with each other in the myth of scarcity and thus maintain its grip on us. We have pretended that things are scarce for so long that we believe they are. We don't question it. Every money guru's advice is based on the unspoken assumption that money is scarce. Time management experts give advice based on the assumption that there is a finite amount of time. We make requests of others out of the belief that our resources are limited.

THIS IS FALSE. THERE IS ENOUGH. THE PEOPLE IN YOUR LIFE HAVE UNLIMITED CAPACITY TO FULFILL ANY REQUEST YOU MAKE OF THEM.

I've noticed that when I ask people for a contribution coming from abundance they often give five to ten times as much as they used to when I operated from scarcity. Also, they are happier with me and more satisfied with their contributions. This breakthrough is available to you in this book.

Here's what I mean by asking for money: asking for a raise; asking for a gift; asking for a loan; asking for an allowance; asking for a pledge, if you are fundraising; asking for a job with a particular salary; asking others to pay your fee or buy your product; asking for venture capital; etc..

We don't see you and your friends as limited, but as possessing unlimited resourcefulness and creativity. We create every dollar we have, whether it is by working, inheriting or winning the lottery. We live in a sufficient world. There is no logical reason for us to compete with each other or to divide ourselves into the "haves" and the "have-nots". Somehow we've got the notion that we don't create our own money but rather that we have fought and sacrificed and toiled for every hard-earned dollar. Our explanation is that someone else -- a boss, parent, government, God -- creates money and we have to manipulate and maneuver to get it. So when we happen to get some "extra", we hold onto it. We build our pile. Wealth accumulation for personal security is a primary goal in our culture.

Constructing a mountain of money and possessions may appear worthwhile but it doesn't accomplish anything in terms of action. To the contrary, it's like plaque (blockages) accumulating in the arteries. It slows one down, stops the circulation of money, which I prefer to think of as energy. The more I accumulate, the more I have to worry about losing it to thieves, blackmailers, incompetent advisors, unsound investments and dependent associates.

iv

Someone said that money is like fertilizer – if you pile it up it stinks – but if you spread it around things get produced.

People like me who give away large amounts of money, particularly if they don't have savings, retirement funds and investments, are considered to be slightly insane by financial advisors. It seems to me that true freedom from money would come from recognizing that we create it all and if we lose it or consciously give it away, we can create it all over again. My own experience, out of giving hundreds of thousands of dollars to charity, is one of unprecedented power and freedom. I am lighter, more flexible, and constantly looking for the next challenge, so I can have yet another opportunity to express my talents and create money.

My experience has been that the more money I direct towards my commitments, the more powerful and effective I become as a generator of money.

This book is not a "how to" guide in the sense of telling you how to get rich quick, how to maximize investments or retire early although such results are possible by-products of freedom from money. This book operates in an entirely different domain – that of context, as opposed to content. Context is like a framework that holds ideas, actions and circumstances rather than the contents themselves. In this case I'm designing a new context or paradigm* in which to hold (relate to) money. This new context provides a new frame through which to view money and the things money can buy.

I say it is completely unnecessary to be seduced and dominated by money. We think we live in a narrow money space. We operate with money as if there are walls and a low ceiling. Einstein, in the following quote refers to this as a prison. I agree that we have deluded ourselves into believing we are in solitary confinement.

"A human being is a part of the whole called by us "Universe," a part limited in time and space. He experiences himself, his thoughts and feelings as something separated from the rest – a kind of optical delusion of his consciousness. This delusion is a kind of prison for us, restricting us to our personal desires and to affection for a few persons nearest to us. Our task must be to free ourselves from this prison by widening our circle of compassion to embrace all living creatures and the whole of nature in its beauty." Albert Einstein.

You can break out of this imaginary prison by reading this book and taking the actions correlated with financial emancipation. You and I can alter our lives forever in an instant. Complete mastery takes hard work, but the payoff is exhilarating. It's called freedom from money, the context of sufficiency.

I'd like to acknowledge a number of my supporters who have made this book a reality.

Thank you to Lee, my wife, for being my loving partner in making financial transformation possible, Jane Bonin, my first editor, my son Rhett, for being straight with me, Harry Benson, for his publishing guidance, Lynne Twist for being my ongoing inspiration, cheerleader, and editor, Duncan and Beebe Nelson, for their editing and many of my friends for urging me to make these ideas public.

Last, but not least, I acknowledge you for engaging in an inquiry about your own relationship to money via this book.

* Paradigm: "A set of rules and regulations that: 1) describes boundaries; and 2) tells you what to do to be successful within those boundaries. A paradigm tells you that there is a game, what the game is, and how to play it successfully."

Joel Barker, Discovering the Future, the Business of Paradigms.

CHAPTER 1

WHO I AM AND WHY I WROTE THIS BOOK IN THE HUMAN RACE, WE NEED TO RUN TOGETHER...

Since 1960 I have been in the financial services industry -- advising people about their savings, investments and insurance. In this capacity I've worked with thousands of people on money matters, my clients ranging from multi-millionaires to people with very modest incomes.

I've helped them to balance their budgets, borrow money, get promoted, start businesses, and plan their estates. I've done this by listening to my clients -- to their hopes and their fears, their joys and their sorrows, their breakdowns and their breakthroughs. I like working for them; I particularly like working *with* them.

Along the way I've had my own money problems. It took me a while to get going in the insurance business. But I've been earning over $150,000 a year on a gross of between $250,000-300,000 for many years. That's more than most people in the financial services industry bring in, though far

1

below the income of the giants of this industry.

In 1978, I started giving money to The Hunger Project; a strategic organization committed to ending hunger through empowering hungry people all over the world to end their own hunger. In 1980, the year I married Lee, we gave more money to The Hunger Project than we had given in total to charities up to that point. This was all the more remarkable given that for twenty years I had been a fund raiser for my church, for my son's private school, for my Rotary Club, for my YMCA Men's Club, and for a number of other charities.

Since we've been married, Lee and I have given over $600,000 to The Hunger Project and we're still going strong. Some years our contribution was as high as $100,000, in others as low as $5,000.

In 1981 I became a volunteer fundraiser for The Hunger Project, and in that capacity I have raised over ten million dollars. I have also helped to train thousands of fundraisers in this country, as well as in England, Canada, Australia, Germany, Austria, Japan, and India.

I've had thousands of one-to-one conversations and I've led hundreds of meetings in this and other countries. In these conversations and meetings I have asked people for money -- lots of money – and, in this context, the people with whom I've engaged have been willing to examine their attitudes towards money. Overwhelmingly their attitudes reflect a culture of scarcity. Our practices of accumulating and consuming are consistent with the cultural belief that:

THERE'S NOT ENOUGH TO GO AROUND

This attitude, this belief, leads to our lack of freedom with money. It is the context for almost all opinion of the economy and almost all advice about personal finances.

But when one creates a context of sufficiency, a context that there *is* enough to go around, one begins to see resources that were not apparent within a context of scarcity. This book is not about succeeding within the present condition of scarcity. It's not about tips and techniques to help people cope with their money problems. This book is about my claim that there is enough to go around. And in support of this claim I will be offering, as an example of this model of sufficiency, the way I am living my life.

These past two decades of self-discovery on my part, in the context of giving and raising sums of money I had not dreamed possible, has been my training for the writing of this book. It has opened up new ways for me to relate to and operate with money. (I share this with you out of my commitment to all of us having access to the freedom and resourcefulness that I experience in my relationship to money.)

A personal financial advisor has a uniquely privileged position from which to address the subject of this book. In "Money And The Meaning Of Life", Professor Jacob Needleman suggests that in our time the insurance agent, the financial planner, and the trust officer have moved into the roles formerly held by the clergyman, the physician, and the psychiatrist. It is the money people, he tells us, that are now privy to people's secret lives -- their anxieties and desires, their shames and sorrows.

Needleman tells of a conversation with one of his "money students," an accountant, who says, "When I see someone's financial records -- or lack of them -- I'm seeing more about them than I want to see. I'm seeing their lies, their contradictions, their hypocrisies, their sexual hang-ups, their hatreds and pettiness, their phenomenal cruelties and their incredible wishful thinking."

If I had written a book after my first twenty years in this business, it would have been about the sorts of things the accountant in Dr. Needleman's class saw -- people's selfishness and inconsistency, their spite and hypocrisy. But my twenty years as a successful fundraiser have opened me up to another dimension -- to people's generosity and creativity.

I've been privileged to be with people at those special times when they've had breakthroughs in their relationship to money, when they have become heroes. We've laughed and cried together out of the joy of funding a project designed to have the world work for every human being. I have chosen to use my energy, my money, my connections, my time, and my talents to work towards ensuring a healthy and productive life for every person on this planet.

I don't know what it's going to take to pull this off, but I'm not willing to hold anything back in the quest. So consider me a champion for you and for your family. And I'm battling for your neighbors, your friends -- and for those you may consider your enemies. I'm particularly fighting for the children of the world, for future generations.

The specific gift I offer you is in the domain of money. In this book I will be constantly inviting you to shift the way in which you relate to money. Much of the suffering and frustration we experience comes from our perception of money as a cure-all, and as such, an end in itself. I say it is far more powerful to perceive it as a tool, as a means towards a much more vital and valuable end.

When you relate to money as an expression of your commitments, your whole world will change. It is our attachment to money and the fact that our lives revolve around it which restricts the movement available to us. Relating to money as a means can give you power; relating to it as an end gives money power over you. Seeing this distinction opens up the choice.

I am using every forum available to me, including this book, to create a new way of thinking and acting with money -- to create new distinctions, new practices, a new money paradigm. The existing paradigm has just about run its course; it's not much use to us anymore.

I'm using a paradigm to mean an unquestioningly (and

unconsciously) absorbed set of rules and beliefs. Within a particular paradigm people react similarly to certain issues. We don't have to think to act within a paradigm; everybody knows what to do. If you stop and examine a paradigm, you can see the rules. They are not so much good or bad rules -- they are simply the rules in force. And, in many ways, the rules limit the game. As I have said, in the current paradigm for money the rules and practices are consistent with the principle of scarcity.

Within an existing paradigm there are ways of thinking and feeling that affect one's course of action. For example, if you lose your job during tough economic times, you may not work hard at getting another job. Economic recessions are characterized by a mood of resignation. Why knock yourself out? Only a fool goes for it when there's no chance. However, if you don't buy into the existing beliefs, if instead you create new thought patterns, you can get the job of your dreams even in hard times.

Ever since I shifted my own paradigm around money, I have been able to assist many other people to fund what is important to them. For the last twenty years I've lived in a reality totally different from my own former reality about money. I've had the good fortune to be able to interact with and learn from people who use money as an expression of freedom and possibility. This book has as its source my experiences with these people, the people who first asked me to contribute substantial money to fund my vision, then trained me to encourage others to contribute. Many of them are now my clients; most are my friends. Together we continue to create this new reality -- a freedom from being dominated by money or the lack of it.

I'm committed to a world free from hunger, pollution, war, crime, and prejudice ... a world that works for everyone. Giving and raising a lot of money to fund my commitments -- more money than I ever thought possible in my wildest dreams -- has freed me from my own "scarcity thinking". I'm committed to sharing my transition in a way that enables you to use money powerfully. I don't want anything *from* you -- I want something *for* you. In the next chapter, I'll talk more about that something *for* you, and I'll also be making some bold and unreasonable promises to you.

CHAPTER 2

MY PROMISES TO YOU

If you stay with the inquiry of this book you will become a new person with money. "They" won't control you anymore. You know "they" -- the Joneses you have been trying to keep up with, the folks on Madison Avenue, the gurus of Wall Street. Any frustration, invalidation, and intimidation you have experienced will diminish or disappear. If you participate powerfully with this book, you will release yourself from that paradigm of personal powerlessness.

The life available to you is incomparably more rewarding than the life you have now. And you can get into it right away!

You can be a pioneer in this new paradigm for money, a pioneer in employing the new distinctions, a pioneer in realizing the advantages gained in sharing these distinctions with others.

Later in this book I will ask you to create a purpose for your money, a purpose for your career. When you behave purposefully, you give your money and your career power.

You invest your money and your career with energy. You begin to move with velocity and force.

You won't be so hesitant about borrowing money yourself, and you won't be so judgmental of borrowers. You'll have a new appreciation for banks and for individuals who lend money.

You'll lighten up about money. Money will not be this deadly serious and burdensomely significant issue for you.

You'll have a new and happier relationship with your job, whatever your job. You'll look forward to getting up and going to work.

You will sleep better. I do! All that tossing and turning is over for me.

You may well find that you're not smoking, drinking, or taking drugs any longer.

You will find that contributing time, talent, and money to something you are committed to will shift from being a burden to being a benefit. As a contributor, a *major* contributor, I'm having a ball! I think of myself as a philanthropist. I *like* it when people ask me for large contributions. It means that they're enthusiastic about their cause, and it means that they see me as someone capable of a generous gift. It now shows up as an acknowledgment of my power.

When I get behind something, I invest a lot of money in it. I gravitate to people and organizations that relate to me as creative and resourceful. And I research organizations and projects to ensure that my money is working well, gives me leverage and is working for what I want.

In 1990 my wife and I made a pledge of $100,000 to The Hunger Project. We didn't know where we were going to get this money; it certainly wasn't in our income forecast. But because we are deeply committed to ending hunger, somehow deep inside we knew we could count on ourselves to create the money.

To put this pledge in perspective, in '88 we had contributed $6,000, and in '89 we had contributed $12,000. When we made the pledge of $100,000, we had no new circumstances -- no inheritance forthcoming, no windfalls, no sales explosions in our insurance business. All we had was our commitment and our ability to create. Not only did we fulfill our commitment; we paid our pledge in full three months early.

I suggest that love and money are connected. Remember, when I say money I mean all that money buys as well, all our material possessions. When you begin to use money creatively rather than possessively, as an expression of passion rather than as an exploitation of power, your intimate relationships will improve dramatically.

CHAPTER 3

THE WAY IT IS NOW

"Someday you'll look back on this and it will all seem funny."
- Bruce Springstein, "Rosalita"

Money was created as a medium of exchange to facilitate trade. It allows us to convert our productivity into a common commodity that we exchange for the results of others' productivity. For example, money enables the farmer to get his boots repaired even when the cobbler isn't in need of corn. Can you imagine how cumbersome it would be, given the plethora of goods produced throughout the world, to continue operating within the barter system? We created money to replace this system. Money was, and still is, a useful invention.

BUT WE GOT OFF THE TRACK

SOMEWHERE ALONG THE WAY WE FORGOT WHY WE CREATED MONEY. WE BECAME ATTACHED TO IT, MADE IT SIGNIFICANT, AND BEGAN TO WORSHIP IT.

We have become addicted to money and the things we buy with it -- jewelry, homes, vacations, land, cars, and education. We fight for it on many battlefields. We are mugged and beaten while holding on to it. We argue over it in divorce court.

On a global scale we kill each other for money, for land, for oil, for food, for diamonds. Most of the wars have been about defending or acquiring land, which could grow food or yield oil and precious metals. For centuries we have sent our children out to kill "their" children for some perceived material advantage for some national interest. In the book *Critical Path*, Buckminster Fuller gives a version of history very different from the one I was taught in school. Fuller tells us that greed and fear have dominated and directed the development of our planet for centuries.

Humans hoard money and attach it to themselves in one form or another: multiple luxury cars, multiple homes, multiple wardrobes. There's nothing wrong with making a lot of money, but what we are doing with our money indicates to me the lack of any real purpose.

Nobody says you *have* to have a purpose for your money, but when you don't, money can become all-important in itself, to the point where people actually take their own lives because of its loss. We remember what happened during the stock market crash of 1929. And the same thing repeats itself whenever financial markets crash. Our addiction to money means that we consider whatever we can get hold of as ours and we do anything to hold on to it.

More and more people cheat on their taxes these days, and many others aggressively challenge the system so as to lessen, or even avoid, their obligations. There is a whole industry devoted to showing us how to pay less in taxes. And many in this industry take the position that people should use any means possible, however questionable, to get out of paying taxes. They justify this attitude by pointing to corruption and mismanagement in government. We're not getting enough value for our tax dollars, they say; or, "I don't like some of the things the government spends my money on --welfare, maybe, or defense.

Will Rogers said: "The income tax has made liars out of more Americans than golf." The fact that most of us are not thrilled to pay taxes is one of the main reasons I wrote this book. There is no need to feel burdened by paying taxes. You and I deserve to benefit in every way from the things on which we spend our money. When my tax bill comes, I choose to feel nurtured by paying this money. I now see my taxes as enabling my government to implement the programs our representatives have designed and ratified to serve us.

With an attitude that it's a *privilege* to pay taxes comes a new relationship with government. You are now declaring your partnership with your government. You may be pleasantly surprised when your letters and calls, coming from partnership, not criticism, are answered.

From another perspective, when money has no purpose beyond itself, we aren't naturally responsible for it. But money doesn't only represent value -- the corn or the shoe repair -- it also represents a contract. When I borrow or loan, sell or pay, I am confirming a promise.   Take the subject of bankruptcy. How do you feel when someone who owes you money declares bankruptcy? Suppose it's a lot of money! Under U.S. law we can declare bankruptcy and then magically erase our debts if we have no assets. Suddenly we don't owe the people we once owed. Even though it's the law, does it empower us to renege on our responsibilities?

About fifteen years ago I loaned a friend $2,500 which he promised to pay back within a year. His financial situation immediately worsened and after a few years he declared bankruptcy. Under our bankruptcy laws his debt to me was legally canceled. However, my friend insisted that he would pay me back someday, plus interest. He sounded sincere. But if he didn't fulfill on his intention I'd be out a few thousand dollars. I could have used that money to fund my commitments.

From time to time my friend let me know he was thinking of his debt to me. Though he and his wife were going through tough times, I realized I wasn't entitled to repayment in a legal sense but he was operating out of his personal standard of integrity so I figured I could count on him. This is atypical in bankruptcies. Most people hide behind the law to get out of paying past debts.

A few years ago he died unexpectedly. His widow paid me back out of the life insurance money. She didn't have to but her integrity and her healthy relationship to money carried the day.

I could have forgiven the debt, but if I did would she be left empowered? I doubt it. If I related to her as a poor widow how would she be left? Today we have a clean and wonderful relationship. Perhaps it's because I refused to relate to her as weak or unable. I would have forgiven the debt, if it had empowered her. Too often people let others off the hook because they don't think they're able to fulfill on their obligations. This is analogous to enabling an addict, keeping him or her weak and dependent.

A banker once told me that of the sixty or seventy people to whom his bank loaned money, who subsequently had gone bankrupt, only three had repaid the excused debt. What do you think the statistics are nationally? How do you feel about this matter?

If I ever go bankrupt, not only will I pay off every debt *with interest*, even though by law I'm not legally obligated, but I will also feel good about doing it! Remember that I said we all stand to benefit from everything for which we spend time or money. Spending money to pay off debts can be thrilling and empowering rather than discouraging and defeating. If you have problems with this way of thinking, consider that your opinions come from the current paradigm of scarcity.

You can probably see how our laws regarding bankruptcy are consistent with the paradigm of scarcity, that they are not designed to give us freedom and power. As you examine more and more of our customs, rules, laws, and beliefs, you will see why we act the way we do with money. Bankruptcy laws allow us to avoid being responsible. And responsibility is power.

MONEY GURUS

GET RICH QUICK! There are many money gurus giving pitches in newspapers, magazines and books, on radio and TV programs, on how to make more money. They use come-ons like: "SAVE 50% ON YOUR INCOME TAXES -- HOW TO BECOME A MILLIONAIRE AND STOP WORKING -- INSTANT WEALTH WITHOUT RISK -- MUTUAL FUNDS THAT PAY 35% EVERY YEAR -- GETTING RICH IS THE BEST *REVENGE* -- SECRETS OF CREATING PRIVATE TAX-FREE WEALTH."

Really???

Could it be that these GURUS are giving us what we want, rather than what we need -- salesmen skilled in finding the buyer's "hot button". The principal message that you hear and read daily is all about building your pile, about hoarding.

Are there any gurus who are using their money to fund their commitments to church, school, hospitals or anything that is really important to them? Or are they just getting richer -- holding on to money for dear life. You and I have paid these people for their books, tapes, and seminars. What examples are they setting for us?

Have you ever seen magazine articles where financial experts analyze the budgets of some "typical" families? The families report their current spending and saving patterns. The experts suggest improvements like putting more money into an IRA, cashing in a CD to put that money in a mutual fund, paying off credit card debt, etc. A typical family gives 1% to 3% of its income to church or charity. I've never seen a magazine article wherein a financial expert suggests that people increase their charitable contributions to the 10% level or higher.

The experts advice implies that: 1) money is limited and finite -- what you have will not expand much; 2) you should hold on to as much of it as you can and; 3) you shouldn't take chances because you could lose everything, and then life wouldn't be worth living. These are some of the basic tenets of scarcity. It's not that the total amount of money is thought to be in short supply but rather that "they" have a disproportionate amount of it.

Following are six examples of how we Americans are run by scarcity:

1 - LAWSUITS IN AMERICA

We are suing each other more than ever. Everything is the other guy's fault -- especially if the other guy has money. We really think we are justified in our attempt to get "them" to pay for our pain and suffering.

I've talked to some Europeans who are amused at this American phenomenon. Doesn't anyone ever cause his own accident? What if we had to pay for court costs and opposing lawyers' fees if we lost? What if our lawyers had to share that cost with us?

When we sue big businesses, including our own doctors, they turn right around and raise the price of their products and services. Somehow, we've got it wired up that it's not fair that rich people, or companies, or the government have deep pockets, and we keep wanting to get into them, on principle as it were, regardless of the counter-productive effects

2 - PRODUCTIVITY OF OUR WORKFORCE

Does money in and of itself really motivate people to be

productive? I think not. It may even be that people are "de-motivated" when money becomes their primary concern. Have you ever seen an athlete go into a prolonged slump right after signing the dream contract? If your boss doubled your salary, would that motivate you to double your output in return? Think about that one.

Many employers have a common gripe. Why don't *they* (the employees) work like *we* do. Why don't they work late? Why are they late coming in to work? Why do they schedule dentist and hairdresser appointments during work time? Why do they call in sick so much? How come they never offer to make up lost time? Why don't they care when the company's revenues fall off? Or if sales drop?

Here's a clue to that gripe. I say employers often look upon their employees as children, and they complain to other employers just like Mommy and Daddy complained to other parents that their kids were irresponsible. Employees tend to see their employers in a parental role -- as protectors.

3 - WHAT ABOUT RICH PEOPLE?

In her song, "Material World", Tracy Chapman sings, "Call it upward mobility, but you've been sold down the river. Just another form of slavery." Attachment to money stops the big boys too, the Wall Street billionaires, stops them from living full, satisfying, productive lives.

All you have to do is look around you and you'll see what I mean. The news is full of accounts of people who have made their dream come true and then ended up in jail. Many of them were heroes of business and industry.

Isn't it surprising to find out that multi-millionaires are doing things that could have them end up broke and in jail? Can you imagine being brilliant or lucky enough to be worth hundreds of thousands or millions of dollars and then jeopardizing everything you've got to get more? Yet many very rich people are currently doing things that could, and do, result in imprisonment.

In the eighties Ivan Boesky was convicted of insider trading, paid millions of dollars in fines, went to jail and forfeited forever his right to work at the thing he knew best. Then there is Leona Helmsley, the lady who had everything! Whatever she gained from cheating on taxes is dwarfed by the ignominy and ridicule she has fallen heir to. Another multi-millionaire, Michael Millken, used insider information to make a lot of money in the stock market, and went to jail for it.

I'm not saying that people with money and power are necessarily bad or that money makes people bad. However, when we perceive money as an end in itself (as its own bliss), we are more likely to become addicted to it. Conversely, when we see money as a way to serve others, and that there is no scarcity of it, we will use it appropriately.

4 - MARRIAGE AND DIVORCE

Marriage is possibly the greatest partnership opportunity available. Just as a business partnership works best when both partners throw everything into the deal, so does a marriage. Yet an increasing number of couples are entering their partnerships with pre-nuptial agreements. A pre-nuptial agreement is an exception in the social contract, which allows one partner to withhold something from the other. In so many words, one spouse is saying, "You can't have all of me and mine -- I'm not surrendering to you. I'm not in the deal 100%." The spouse who accepts this is ripe for the role of "victim." I say that this is a contradiction to the intention of the marriage vows. I've always doubted that there can be full self-expression in these marriages.

Money discussions in marriages are usually avoided until absolutely necessary because they carry such a high emotional charge. We read that money or the lack of it is the chief cause of arguments in marriage. My wife and I fell into this trap early in our marriage but, with some expert coaching, designed a purpose for the money that flows through us – to use it in the service of society-wide transformation.

Many marital money arguments are never resolved. People just get tired and stop arguing. As a result, disappointment, invalidation and hurt spills over into every area of the relationship.

5 - RETIREMENT

Some people can't wait to retire. For years a number of my contemporaries have been saying: "I'm almost done." "It won't be long." "I've paid my dues." "I'm taking it easy." "I'm outta here."

The dictionary tells us retiring is withdrawing, retreating. From what? Often not from work that brings pride and satisfaction, but rather from work seen as a struggle, a necessary evil. Chances are if you were offered retirement now, with a guarantee of the same life style, you'd jump at it. Another definition from Webster's: "Retire -- to give ground, as in battle. Retiring -- drawing back from contact with others." What if work were enormously satisfying and thrilling? Would we be tired? Would we want to withdraw? Imagine what we bring to our jobs when our attitude is, "I'd quit today if I could afford to." Maybe that's why many corporations offer attractive early retirement programs. They're interested in getting the deadwood out and bringing in new people eager to contribute. Maybe your boss would make a bigger profit by paying you to stay home.

6 - DISABILITY CLAIMS

The insurance industry has never seen anything like these last few years. Disability insurance claims have gone through the roof. Individual disability insurance policies are designed to pay out 50 to 60 cents in claims on the average for every dollar paid in. For much of the nineties many leading insurance companies have been paying claims at the rate of 80 to 150 cents on the dollar.

Given our attitude towards work and employers, the prospect of not having to work and getting paid nearly as much money in insurance benefits as we earned in salary is very tempting.

As a result of this deluge of disability claims, many insurance companies dropped out of the disability insurance market. Others increased their rates for new policies, fired insurance agents who had too many clients collecting benefits, tightened their claim practices, scaled down benefits offered in new policies and generally made it tougher for people to buy disability insurance.

When I tell other insurance agents that professionalism in the insurance industry has declined, they become extremely defensive. Most agents who sell life and disability insurance are more interested in getting the sale and keeping the customer than in talking straight and putting the client's needs first.

SUMMARY

You and I live in a world where we've made money more important than people. In the pursuit of money and the things money buys, important standards have been compromised. Our attachment to money interferes with our relationships, our job satisfaction, and ultimately our freedom. Greed poses perhaps the greatest danger to our planet, greed expressed in everything from the destruction of rain forests to the exploitation of child labor. Much of the world looks to the United States for models of both moral and economic stability. Our practices are far more influential than we suspect. If we can only see how costly it is to relate to money the way we do, we will make a contribution to people in many other countries. It is time for new values and fresh expressions of old ones, as we come to the final days of the millennium and anticipate the ages to come.

CHAPTER 4

MORE ABOUT THE WAY IT IS NOW

*"The mass of men lead lives of quiet desperation. What is
called resignation is confirmed desperation."*
> - Henry David Thoreau, *Walden*

I am going to suggest something and ask that you try it on for
size.

You cannot get enough money. What looks like enough today
won't be enough tomorrow. Whatever you get, you'll go for
more.

There's a young man I know who has already built a net worth
of over three million dollars. He recently acknowledged me and
my wife for giving $100,000 to The Hunger Project in a single
year then told us, "I'm going to do that someday, too." That
"someday" would come when he felt he had enough for
himself. Out of that interaction I began to consider: how *do* we
know when we have enough for ourselves so we can start
giving away to others? And I saw that as long we live in a
condition of scarcity, we can never have enough!

Notice how people buy boats, then buy bigger boats. Then they buy a yacht. Then a bigger yacht. Try to talk to a boat owner about his boat and you'll find he wants to talk about his next boat.

This pervasive feeling of insufficiency -- "not big enough," "not fast enough," "not luxurious enough" -- keeps us reaching out for more. It's a condition I've talked about before, a condition called scarcity. We live and breathe in this condition of scarcity as we live and breathe in the condition of oxygen -- unconsciously and without awareness. In a condition of scarcity, there's not enough to go around, so everyone is a threat to everyone else.

To feel insufficient is also to feel incomplete, to feel that your life is missing some things. Once you have these things, you think, you'll be complete. You can't let up until you get the right car, the right clothes, the right TV, the right vacation -- the right "stuff." Only you find that as you get more stuff, there's always more to get.

For many of us the goal is to have enough money so that we won't have to work. And we want to get enough before we're too old to work, or before someone tells us we're too old to work. The American dream is early retirement.

But how can we attain financial independence and job security in a world where things are scarce? Prices go up. Younger and smarter people enter the job market. New and confusing technology changes all the rules. The Pacific Rim countries are taking over our markets. It's scary, this scarcity. There are not enough jobs and there are too many people seeking them.

Suppose you're thirty-five years old with a wife and two kids, ages three and eight. You earn $45,000 and you've peaked. Any income increases from now on will be tied to the cost of living index. What are your worries? Tight cash flow? Little or no savings? Kids costing more and more as they grow? In a few years you'll have to confront orthodontist bills -- and in ten years your oldest will start college. One kid will be out for a year and then the other enters. When your youngest graduates you'll be 54, only eleven more years to retirement. And remember you'll have to pay for a wedding if you have a daughter.

There's enough worry right there to keep you awake nights. And then you think, "Will I have to help out my folks? What if my wife gets sick? What if I get sick?" Talk about quiet desperation. Is it any wonder people drink too much, get divorced, use drugs?

Look at another scenario: a couple approaching sixty, kids out of the nest. Health care costs are soaring. Where should they be investing? Savings and loans? Mutual funds? Municipal bonds? What if one of the kids has it rough and moves back home? How much money do they need to retire and *live the good life?*

The belief that things are scarce dominates all our thinking. It keeps us on the defensive, protecting, hoarding, holding on. We become stingy. Notice how you feel in a traffic jam when a car cuts in front of you -- like you lost something. That's scarcity. Not enough time to get where you're going, not enough time to deal with the demands once you get there.

Each year in January we're hit with credit card bills from the holiday season. And it's time to start assembling our ammunition to fight the income tax return wars. What a way to begin the new year! Then the guy from your favorite charity calls you up to ask how much they can expect from you this year. He's hoping you'll give much more; you're wondering if you should pledge at all. There isn't enough to take care of everyone. Isn't this the year that it was all going to turn out?

Now the insurance man calls, reminding you that you told him to call after the first of the year. How much will *this* cost? Maybe you can keep putting him off. Is buying more life insurance the way to go? Who's living this Great American Dream you hear so much about? Better go buy a few lottery tickets! But there are not enough winning numbers and there are too many players. Scarcity again, and again...and again.

We believe that EVERYTHING is scarce -- money, property, time, love. We operate as if there is only so much money, so we get ours first and hold onto it. "There's only so much to go around so I've got to get mine." This kind of behavior leads to stress and emotional suppression, not only for you but for your loved ones as well.

I say that the condition of scarcity is so thick and so solid "in our experience" that it has become an unquestioned reality. You haven't had enough sleep, you don't have enough time, you don't have enough money, and you're not getting enough love. Anyone you talk to will agree with you about scarcity.

My friend, Lynne Twist, Chair of the State of the World Forum's Board of Directors, says that the lightning rod around which this condition of scarcity crystallizes is the assumption that there is not enough money. She points out that everyone, no matter what his or her economic level, feels damaged around money. "They are wounded," she says, "they are bruised, they are hurt.... It is going to take a while for the wounds to heal. Money is the place where we confront hardest and most painfully that there is not enough.... The way to work on scarcity is to work on the area of money."

SCARCITY LEADING TO CRIME

More Americans are behind bars today than ever before. Our country has the highest number of prisoners per capita in the world. This increase in crime and imprisonment is another symptom of the condition of scarcity, the condition that has us think we need something the other guy has got. I call it "either/or" thinking. It's either him or me. Conversely, if we experienced ourselves as sufficient, whole, complete, resourceful, independent, not in need of anything, who among us would steal? I suggest that our petty, miserly, and covetous behavior comes from our forgetting our sufficiency, forgetting who we really are.

COVETOUSNESS AT THE CORPORATE LEVEL

Big corporations play the "getting" game at a sophisticated level. They want what you've got and they hire the brightest people in America to help them get it -- the Madison Avenue advertising companies. And they get us to give them our money for the damnedest things -- wine coolers, video cameras, cigarettes, luxury cars, beauty aids, sneakers for every occasion. "Just Do It!" means "Just Buy It!"

A FOUNDATION OF INTEGRITY

Report after report shows that the younger generation (18 to 30) has significantly less integrity than the previous generation. Kids cheat on tests more than ever and without remorse. The main goal of college students seems to be learning how to make money. The need to make money, get ahead, have material things, seems to be driving everything these days. As long as going for the bucks is dominant, we are probably going to see even more people in jail.

A few years ago we hired a highly recommended consultant for our business. We hired him to coach us to produce a breakthrough in productivity. We were looking for a 50% to 100% increase. After a few months of working together, he concluded that a breakthrough in sales would not make any difference to us. He noticed that we spent all the money we made even in our best years. We consistently spent more than we'd made by using credit lines and loans. He called this "mortgaging our future."

Our consultant pointed out that breakthroughs in productivity would not be available to us unless we established a foundation of integrity with money. He suggested that we learn to live within our income. This was bad news because we wanted *more* money, not less. We *needed* more money. We still didn't have our boat and our second home. He pointed out that we would always need more money unless we developed better habits. At the time we were giving ourselves eight to ten weeks of vacation a year. Every course we wanted to take we'd simply sign up for. I had a new Jaguar XJS and my wife had a new BMW convertible. He said that our addictions were running us and that more money wasn't the answer. To ensure that our business would be profitable we had to stop "raiding the till."

I was so angry with him I was ready to cancel our consulting contract. We had signed him on to help us get more money and it looked to me like he had failed us. But after Lee and I discussed his advice over a number of days, we began to appreciate its value.

We began to see that we already had enough money, enough things, and that the mad scrambling for more derived from our scarcity thinking. We saw that in order to increase our sales we first needed to learn to live within our income. We saw that if we made a million dollars, but spent $1.2 million, we'd be in the same leaky boat. We recommitted to working with him. He asked us to design a realistic budget. I hated it at first. But within six months we were in control of our buying compulsions. I now look back on his consulting as a milestone in the development of our financial maturity. It enabled us to break the stranglehold of our addictions.

THE MYTH THAT TIME IS SCARCE

We also think that *time* is scarce. Is there enough time for the exercise you need? Enough time for your family? Enough time for your career? Enough time for reading? On my vacations I used to spend a lot of time taking side trips after I arrived at my destination, even though the purpose of my vacation was rest and relaxation. "I've come this far," I'd be thinking. "I may never get a chance to come back. I don't want to miss anything." And in trying not to miss anything, I'd miss out on my vacation.

RETIREMENT

People are concerned about saving for their old age. Some people are so governed by this concern that they put aside a disproportionate amount of income for early retirement. But who says one ever has to stop working? I intend to work until I drop. Don't get me wrong. There's good reason to save for a time when work may be impossible. But actions motivated out of scarcity are not powerful. When we save money for the future at the expense of fully participating in the present, we cheat ourselves of the fullness of life. When your church, for example, asks you to increase your contribution, you may reply that you can't because you're saving for retirement. It's likely that your place of worship has played a central role in your life. You grew up in it, got married in it, raised your kids in it, and now you acknowledge and recommend it to many people. Yet you've been so conditioned to think "either/or" that you can't see how *both* your money and your church are integral to your retirement, even as they have been integral to your life.

The columnist Andy Rooney did a piece on retirement, which pointed out how many people wanted to stop working. He noted a statistic that showed that in one year 84% of all employees working for large companies with pension plans opted to retire before they reached age 65. Voluntarily! Imagine how negative their experience of working must have been.

A GOOD TIP!

Another "condition of scarcity" situation is the agonizing over how much to tip service providers. Having to deal with our stinginess has ruined many a good meal. When the bill comes and you have to figure out the tip, do you get weird? Is the percentage of your tip related to the service you get? Consider this: the service you get may be related to your "prevailing attitude" of cheapness. It may be that your waiter or waitress can "smell" how small your tip is going to be right away. I suspect that the reason I almost always get superb service is because I've decided *before* the meal that I'm going to tip handsomely. Worth a try.

TRUST IN OURSELVES

The condition of scarcity deprives us of trust in ourselves, deprives us of freedom and power. Can you promise to give away money you don't have? Can you make a pledge that is beyond your ability to fulfill? Most people can't. Suppose you earn $50,000 a year and all of it is accounted for. Could you pledge $10,000 to a charity and trust yourself to go out and create it? If you say yes, I challenge you to pick up the phone right now and make that pledge to something that's important to you. Most people get very uncomfortable when I ask them to consider pledging an amount over and above what they expect to make.

What's the truth about your unwillingness to give a lot of money away? Do you think you can't? Don't you trust yourself to create whatever you need? Do you fear being ridiculed if you fail? Are you afraid that your peers will laugh at you for being conned? If so, you're not the only one. Look around you and you'll see a lot of people stopped by these reasons.

I'm pointing to the lack of trust people have in themselves. When you pledge money do you trust yourself enough to honor your pledge? Are you stingy with yourself? This is different than living beyond one's means. This is creating one's future beyond one's history. You can actually alter the future by cultivating trust in yourself.

HUMANITYOR PROPERTY?

Are you giving up your life for money? Would you literally give up your life for money? If a guy stopped you with a gun demanding your wallet, your jewelry, and your watch, would you give them up? Or would you risk your life for your stuff? Do you have a gun in your house to defend your stuff?

I used to patronize a gas station owned by one of my clients. One day, while I was getting gas, my client was talking about a robbery at a local business. "If anybody tried to rob me," he said, "I'd kill him." I was taken aback, and I asked him if he carried a pistol. "Hell, yes," he said. He pulled one out and waved it around. We talked for a while. He was not open to the notion that a person's life was worth more than a few hundred dollars. I changed gas stations and he changed insurance agents.

Have you sold out on a career you love in order to make money? Have you put your vision on hold because you haven't found a way to make enough money doing what's in your heart? When people are dragging themselves to work, it's a sure sign that their work is a means to an end rather than an expression of their vision. Bucky Fuller often said that if everyone did the kind of work or play that they loved to do, things would sort out perfectly. I suspect he's right.

Another instance of "selling out" revealed itself in the disability insurance coaching classes our business was conducting. The coach I had hired to work with the agents one to one in increasing their productivity while taking care of their clients reported that they seemed suppressed. There was no passion for what they were doing. When she asked them why they were in the insurance business, many said that it was a good way to make a living. This attitude showed in the choice of products they were selling and in the choice of people to whom they were selling these products. Instead of calling on their natural network of friends, neighbors, and family, they were sending out direct mail and working on referred leads. They basically sold whatever the buyer asked for, rather than taking the time to find out what the buyer needed.

A critical aspect of an insurance agent's job is to function as an advisor. I suggest to my agents that they find out where their prospective clients are headed and guide them in taking actions that will get them there. Many agents sell to the client's preferences and considerations, rather than professionally and firmly advocating that they take actions consistent with their overall objectives in life.

In our conference calls with agents we train, we ask them to define success. We ask them what results, if produced, would have them say that they'd had a successful year. All of them, at least initially, give virtually the same response -- making more money than they had made the year before. We then asked if having their clients in better physical and emotional shape could also constitute success, even if their income stayed about the same. They all agreed that would be nice but not what they would call success. What we were pointing out is the possibility that success can be measured by how many people you serve humanly as well as financially.

What constitutes success in your line of work? How high on your list of objectives is serving people? Is your job all about making a living? It's not surprising that most people are working to make a living rather than working as an exciting and satisfying expression of themselves. Indeed it's thoroughly consistent with scarcity thinking that work devolves into making money.

During the recession in the 80's there were many reports of white-collar crime. Many pillars of the community have turned to crime to support their lifestyle as their incomes fell. Wonderful people can become very low and nasty when their money bottoms out. This can happen to you and those around you. If people believe they *need* homes, cars, vacations, and other trappings, they will do virtually anything to keep these things. In a condition of scarcity the end justifies the means: DO WHATEVER YOU CAN TO GET THE MONEY.

When people are frantic to strike it rich, or win the lottery, their normally good judgment can become clouded. For example, a few years ago the headlines reported a scheme whereby a Ghanain, claiming to be disinherited royalty, said he was entitled to a fortune. This fortune was held, inaccessible, in Swiss banks. He enrolled quite a few "smart" US investors in giving him money to deal with the Swiss legal system, promising a ten to twenty fold return on their investments.

A number of people gave him millions before the whole thing was exposed as a scam. One friend of mine put in several hundred thousand dollars. Greed can suck the best of us into

29

these kinds of schemes. Human beings are sitting ducks for the lure of a lot for nothing, big reward for little risk.

We think we need more money than we have. Perhaps the most telling way I have ever heard it said is this: you can never have enough of what you don't *really* need anyway. How true. The bottomless nature of this trap is that we are insatiable. Our greed, our ravenousness, consumes our lives. While you're trying to get the resources you think you need to live your life, your life is going by. In the condition called scarcity, there is never enough. Never!

In his incisive book, *Getting to the 21st Century*, David Korten points to the difference between "cowboy economics and spaceship economics." A cowboy lives for himself, taking whatever he needs, discarding what no longer serves his needs. This behavior has got the world in the shape it's in.

Spaceship economics underlines our relationship with one another; i.e., "We're all in the same boat". Somebody is always downstream from someone else. When we participate as a global community, all interconnected, we are acknowledging a context of sufficiency, a context wherein no one need take anything from another. Korten writes: "Unless we all come to embrace a vision more consistent with our collective reality, we will suffer dearly in the years ahead." What I'm committed to getting across is that the paradigm of scarcity is costing us dearly right now!

SUMMING UP

Some say we are limited; I say that we are not. Some say there is scarcity; I say there is sufficiency. You can free yourself from your attachment to money. This new paradigm is very easy to access. You don't have to keep suffering.

You really can have a very different future if you can suspend your judgments, specifically your notions about scarcity, and come over here with me for the next eighty pages or so. We'll be looking at life through a different filter.

Let me remind you that we're all in this scarcity condition together. It's a big-time conversation that drives our economy and runs our lives. We're not bad people because we think from scarcity. It's the existing paradigm. All money books I've read are written from this paradigm. They all tell us how to move around better within scarcity. The possibility I'm proposing is that we can stop buying into scarcity. We can stop selling our sufficiency short.

There are many examples of cultures and communities that have operated from sufficiency rather than scarcity. With the unfolding of the modern world, many of these cultures and communities have taken on practices and behaviors consistent with scarcity. This is because they were operating under a circumstantial system of sufficiency rather than an "invented" (created, declared) context of sufficiency, so in entering the modern world they were without resources to protect their heritage.

In her book *Ancient Future*, Helena Norberg-Hodge writes of the simple, beautiful life in Ladakh, an area in the north of India. She had spent much time with these people in the 70's and was disturbed to see how the modern world had brought about so many negative changes upon her return. She writes: "When I first arrived in Ladakh the absence of greed was striking. People were not particularly interested in sacrificing their leisure or pleasure simply for material gain. Development is stimulating dissatisfaction and greed; in so doing, it is destroying an economy that had served people's needs for more than a thousand years. They were satisfied with what they had. But now, whatever they have is not enough."

The Ladakhis cannot return to their old ways. However, they, like you, can create sufficiency while living in the modern world. The dominant condition in our world is scarcity. The way to alter it is to create a context of sufficiency. In a few chapters, you will have access to creating sufficiency on a sustainable basis. This chapter was designed to have you see how frustrating and limiting our attitudes towards money are, as well as to have you get in touch with the cost of these attitudes. I hope you are thoroughly tired of reading it! It's high time to go on to -- or rather to shift over to -- something else: a new paradigm.

CHAPTER 5

WHAT'S MISSING IN THE CURRENT MONEY PARADIGM?

Let's examine an example of a paradigm shift. Up until a few years ago it was impossible for humans to fly (as opposed to glide) without an engine-powered aircraft. Then somebody built a lighter-than-air, man-powered aircraft. A guy or gal could just get in and pedal all around the sky. That's a paradigm shift caused by a breakthrough in technology. It can alter everything.

What if in a short while we will be able to build these bicycle-aircraft from kits. Looks like they won't cost much once the technology really kicks in. The sky will be full of us pedaling around like Mary Poppins. No more reliance on fossil fuels -- no more pollution. People won't be riding to work on subways and buses, won't be spending hours in bumper-to-bumper traffic. The implications of such a paradigm shift in transportation are huge. It could affect the longevity of our planet.

Unimaginable here at the beginning of the twenty-first century?

No more so than airplanes were at the beginning of the twentieth!

In the current paradigm, money is the prize -- the thing to go for. So naturally we organize ourselves around making money. But change the game and everything shifts.

MISSING: EMPOWERMENT

Say you invest money in the stock market, in real estate, in oil wells, and your money doubles. Are you empowered? Do you sleep better? Does your health improve? Are you a better husband or father, wife or mother? Do lines disappear from your face? Are you more alive, more in love with life? Probably for three days at most.

What if we measured the return on an investment by the degrees of improvement in our well being? *What if*, when we put time and/or money into something, we looked for a return of vigor and enthusiasm for ourselves and for those around us.

What if advertisements read, "Put your money in this project and you'll:

1) HAVE MUCH MORE ENERGY AND NEED MUCH LESS SLEEP;
2) END YOUR DEPENDENCY ON PILLS, ALCOHOL, AND CIGARETTES;
3) LOWER YOUR BLOOD PRESSURE AND YOUR WEIGHT;
4) BE MORE ATTRACTIVE TO – AND ATTRACTED TO – THE PEOPLE IN YOUR LIFE;
5) BE MORE TRUSTING AND TRUSTWORTHY?"

Sound like the guy selling snake oil? But suppose there were evidence of the above results in the lives of people you knew. *What if* you could see overwhelming evidence that investing in a particular project or business delivered health and aliveness -- even ecstasy. Wouldn't that make doubling your money pale in comparison?

What if paying taxes left you feeling more related to people in your community and nation?

My contention is that the prevailing perception of income taxes, as an imposition to be evaded however and whenever possible, disempowers and disables our participation as citizens. It doesn't have to be that way. We could be thrilled to pay our taxes. We could see paying taxes as the opportunity, indeed the privilege that it is.

If money was seen as an instrument for getting things done that need to get done, rather than as an instrument dedicated solely to getting mine, we would have a very different relationship with taxes.

What if contributing money to your favorite cause left you with more energy, more sense of sufficiency and well being -- just as vigorous exercise can enhance rather than dissipate your energy? *What if* directing your money into projects benefiting humanity had you locating resources to which you otherwise had no access?

What if by asking to be interacted with as a resourceful person, you actually became one?

I'm saying that you can design yourself as sufficient and resourceful, and that money is what you can use to do it. I know you can do it because I have done it. I have made myself over into a resourceful and powerful person with money. And I used to be a financial wimp.

My history did not indicate that I would ever be powerful with money. If we could assemble the bank officers to whom I have applied for loans over the past 30 years and ask them to present a composite of Les Traband, the borrower, you would not be impressed.

And if we invited to this assemblage the accountants and consultants who have advised me over the years, along with past employees and various credit managers, you would be even less impressed.

One reason I can authentically write this book is that I've been there, have scrambled to keep up with the Joneses, and have gotten thoroughly scarred in the process. I had the big English Tudor house with the underground sprinkler system, the Mercedes and the Jaguar, the cellar full of fine wines. And I had the checks bouncing, the loans to pay off the loans, the sleepless nights wondering how I could pay my bills, the uneasy days trying to keep up the appearance of success.

It was interesting. No matter how much I got, it still wasn't enough. It always generated the need for more.

MISSING: INTEGRITY

Wouldn't it be great if you had financial advisors who were on your side -- competent, trustworthy people with whom you could leave your money and your children's money, and it would all be managed with total integrity, no matter what adversities (financial or otherwise) your advisors might be going through?

Don't bet on it. When times get tough, many advisors go into survival; and in survival they take actions they would never take in normal times -- like taking your money and your children's money. Ask the doctors who have lost millions in investment schemes. Ask the lawyers and accountants who evaluate life insurance programs and investment opportunities being proposed to their clients. You can imagine how many self-serving deals they see as opposed to client-serving deals. I say that only a small percentage of advisors will be really on your side through thick and thin. *What if* this small percentage could become the norm rather than the exception? What will it take to make integrity, rather than survival, our second nature?

IS PARTNERSHIP/RELATEDNESS MISSING IN THE CURRENT MONEY PARADIGM?

What if money could be a game with no losers?

What if you and I could not fail in the domain of money?

What if making money were as unimportant as the score of a friendly softball game? We keep score in friendly games, but the score is not life-and-death, it is not even significant. The score will not interfere with getting a good night's sleep. It will not diminish the love we have for our children.

What if, the casinos were set up so that we couldn't lose more than a sum appropriate for an evening's entertainment? *What if* there was no danger of debilitating loss and destructive addiction, but opportunity only for social enjoyment.

EVERYBODY WINS

What if you and I entered financial transactions only if we could find a win for everyone involved?

Here's a real life example of that kind of transaction. My wife and I sold our office building to free our equity so that we could pay the $64,000 balance on our 1990 Hunger Project pledge of $100,000. Everyone involved in the transaction won.

The new owners wanted our building for a retail store and they felt the price was right. They won us as friends and as customers. So they won. And the town preferred stores to offices, so the town won.

The Hunger Project received payment in full, three months earlier than promised. And they got a terrific story to tell: about a couple who got more value out of investing in the end of hunger than investing in real estate. So the Hunger Project won.

The sale price was high enough to not only pay our pledge balance but also to give us some spending money. We won.

The movers won. The lawyers and title insurance people won.

The real estate firm that made it happen won. We rented an office in a vacant building and our new landlords were happy. The guys who sold and installed the new carpet won. The printing company that sold us new stationery and cards won. We could walk to work, so we reduced to one car and use less fossil fuel. The environment won.

Best of all, we are sharing with others that buying the end of hunger is a better investment than buying real estate, so that other couples and individuals may see that possibility for themselves.

Our intention was to have everybody walk away a winner, and that is exactly what happened.

What if you knew that you would lose big if anyone involved in a deal with you didn't also win? *What if* your first responsibility in any transaction were to make sure there would be no losers?

What if corporations and institutions publicly committed to the welfare of all, for example through committing to the quality of the environment?

What if your employer really acted on your suggestions for the improved well being of employees, customers, and neighbors?

What if there were no such thing in life as a ZERO SUM GAME, a game in which there must be a loser for every winner -- for every plus one, a minus one? *What if* we were to discover that everyone can win, and at no one else's expense?

MISSING: LIVING WITH A PURPOSE

What is a purpose? A purpose arises out of a particular commitment; it is the expression of that commitment. If one has a purpose, one goes about life intentionally, consciously. Purpose is like a compass.

When another agenda crosses our purpose, for example an

agenda like getting approval, we can get distracted. For example, a young man once requested a meeting with me to discuss his idea for a project that could make a major contribution to humanity. He had heard about my success at raising millions of dollars for charity.

His idea sounded fine on the surface, but he was not getting very far with it. He couldn't seem to raise much money, couldn't seem to get other people involved. I asked him some questions that soon revealed his hidden agenda.

He was a dentist who had never made much money, and this project was to be his new career. His intention was to bring in enough money so that he could pay himself an annual salary of $200,000 as the project director. This would enable him to leave dentistry and direct the project full-time.

I asked him if he would be willing to empower the project even if someone else ran it. In other words, *what if* he was to continue practicing dentistry and play a lesser role in the project? He looked at me uncomprehendingly; told me again that this was his future career, his ticket to prosperity.

The point of the story is that the money had become more important to him than the purpose. There's nothing wrong with making a lot of money along the way, but there's something inauthentic about having money take over as the primary objective.

A purpose needs to be shared with others. The more we promote our purpose, the more real it becomes. I am completely committed to ending hunger on this planet as soon as humanly possible. Everyone that I encounter in life soon learns that this is what I'm up to.

At the annual insurance convention hosted by the company to acknowledge its top producers, the Chairman of the Board usually introduces each agent and his or her spouse. He typically lets everyone in the room know each person's sales figures, the length of their time with the company, their years as a sales leader, and something personal about them.

Sometimes he will mention that so-and-so's son is attending a certain college, that so-and-so is building a Jacuzzi or has recently shot a good round of golf. Every time he introduces Lee and me, he publicly acknowledges us for our commitment: "These two people are doing something remarkable; they are ending hunger in the world by giving their own money and by raising a lot of other people's money."

As a result of this type of "free publicity," some of my colleagues now contribute sizable amounts of money to The Hunger Project and many others ask us about The Hunger Project when we see them.

A purpose, properly engaged in, is neither antagonistic nor exclusive. It includes everyone and everything. I am not in agreement with the actions of people and groups in the world like Khadaffi, Saddam Hussein, the Mafia, the Ku Klux Klan, street gangs and terrorists. However, these people and groups are not my enemies. I'm interested in finding ways to have things work for them as well as for you and for me, at no one's expense.

I devote my speaking, my money, and my time to having the world work for everyone. When I stay true to this purpose my actions and decisions come easily into alignment. And because my fundraising projects are joyous and enlivening rather than grim and obligatory, I never have a problem getting volunteers to assist me.

Is it possible that everyone could have the same purpose? *What if* everyone declared a better world for everyone to be the game we were all going to play? What would life be like if we were all committed, as our top priority, to serving others?

What if we competed by seeing who could be the biggest conduit for money? I've always liked the image of being a fireman with money, directing it like water from a powerful hose towards where it is most needed.

Many charitable groups ask people to give until it hurts. I say the opposite: give until it stops hurting! What hurts is not giving enough. Give until you experience yourself as whole and complete. Think of giving as investing; transform yourself from a donor making charitable gestures to an owner of the planet committed to self-reliance for all. Through giving, you will be able to experience your power, your leadership -- and last but not least, your love.

What if we could rid ourselves of that addiction to money I addressed in the earlier chapters?

You are going to see how simple it is to shape the world to match up with all these *what ifs*. You and I and our network of friends and family can create a world that works for everyone, with no one and nothing left out. I have started to live my own life this way, as have others. Let's see if we can adopt large purposes and take win-win actions without making anybody wrong. I say it can be done.

Congratulations on reading this far. You have completed the most difficult part -- the confrontation with how much our scarcity thinking suppresses and limits us.

The rest of this book will give you access to actions that will make sufficiency rather than scarcity your reality. It's heady, fast-moving stuff, so hold tight. Or better yet, *let go*!

CHAPTER 6

THE WAY IT COULD BE

I know you. I know what you complain about, what you want, what you've given up fighting for, what you dream about. We have the same quest. We are on the same side.

This book is about having our lives make a difference. I have promised you quite a lot so far. Now it's time for me to deliver. It's time for you to have a sound night's sleep every night, for you to experience great sex, excellent health, empowering relationships, peace of mind, and a spirit of joy -- as natural.

My wife, Lee, has a commitment to use our relationship as an empowering model for other relationships, and she has helped me to grow into this opportunity. A while back she helped me discover that I'm a show-off. Of course everyone around me had known that. I was the last to find out. When my perception of money began to shift such that I saw the possibility of being free and unattached to it, I wanted more than anything to contribute this freedom to everyone. Being a show off was in the way of my contributing because people wouldn't listen to me. In fact, they got upset; it sounded like I was saying, "I'm better than you. I know everything there is to know about money. Look at me! I'm free!" By implication, I was saying that they were not. What I intended as coaching came across as preaching. My dilemma was this: how could I be true to myself, not pretend I was humble when I wasn't, and still contribute to people?

I am privileged to have participated in a course offered to people who have taken on a seemingly impossible project -- the ending of hunger. The course showed me how I could re-invent myself so as to accomplish this project, using everything I had, *including* being a show-off. For example, I could show off my willingness to be coached, and could get the best coaches and show them off. Once I saw I could *choose* how and what to show off, "showing off" became a resource rather than a drawback, an asset rather than a liability.

RELATIONSHIPS

Wouldn't it be great if people got married, stayed in love, stayed in shape, appreciated each other more and more, and really accomplished something together? Over 50% of marriages in the U.S. end in divorce. And where are the other 50%? In ecstasy?

Weddings are fun; I like going to them. I cry. I laugh. I dance. But I always wonder if anybody has had a talk with the bride and groom about "sickness and health," "richer or poorer." Will they stay around if their spouse gets disabled, disfigured, or files for bankruptcy? Will they keep going full out if "poorer" strikes? Is anybody asking these questions?

Why get married in the first place? Perhaps we find a mate because in our culture it's embarrassing to be single, especially for women. It looks like something's wrong with us. It's no accident that most advertising is directed to having us smell good, look good, and be attractive enough to land a mate.

One of the reasons we give for getting married is because

we're in love with him/her.

Is it possible that "You're the only one for me" is a myth; is it possible that we can create love with anyone?

Another reason we give for marrying is that it will be so great to have the security of a committed partnership. But if we can't stop smoking, lose weight, be on time, and so forth, where do we get off making a lifetime commitment? I wager that most of us think in terms of getting, not giving, when we begin a relationship.

Perhaps we need to look again at our reasons for getting married. Here are some suggestions.

1) To further your mission: If you identify your mission, (a mission being a project that serves others), then your prospective spouse can have something larger than the relationship to support and empower. It's so easy to sell out for the comforts of marriage. If your spouse is not completely on board with you, you may have to carry him/her and your projects could be slowed down or stopped. Why hook up with someone who is not committed to forwarding your mission?

2) To further your partner's mission: Does your partner have a mission? Do you know what it is? Can you get behind it?

3) To further your joint mission: As a unit you could be more powerful than as individuals

4) To have fun: Wouldn't it be exciting to find someone who has a purpose in life, who's up to something big, to which you can contribute?

There is a joy in surrendering to another person -- not surrender like in having lost, more like merging. When you are in touch with your sufficiency, you can surrender to another because you don't need anything from them and you can't lose anything to them. You're available for partnership.

I propose that love is a creation, a way of being. When we are loving, anyone who is in our lives is the beneficiary. Everyone becomes lovable, not as a symbol of success or possession, but as a gift. Perhaps it is the *privilege* of human beings to love one another and, by doing so, to contribute to life.

If you are contributing rather than hoarding, whether it is money or love, fabulous people will participate with you. The chance for a fulfilling marriage is far greater when the partners have a common commitment *beyond the relationship* than when the marriage is founded on the need to look good or to have security.

My wife and I have meetings on a regular basis to recreate the context for our marriage and our money. Basically, we're married to create a new possibility for marriage, to empower others in their relationships, and to use our partnership to end hunger. We're both committed to using our money to fund our commitments and to live in balance. Even with this kind of structure, it's easy for marriages to devolve into soap opera -- drama, gossip, and infidelity. My wife and I are aware of the pull of apathy and resignation and we lean the other way by putting our shoulders into each other's commitments.

A GREAT LOVE LIFE

My wife tells me that women want to be married to men -- not boys. Boys can be fun for a while, but they're not appropriate for marriage. They're interested in themselves and their own pleasures, not the pleasures and passions of their women.

Boys are absorbed in their toys or games no matter how old they are. Boys are constantly showing off for each other. A MAN is focused on serving. Get that one straight, and you have the possibility of both great physical intimacy and great spiritual intimacy.

When a man's life is about contribution, *without self-interest*, he becomes very attractive. When his focus is off himself and on his mate, he can hear her and be open to her.

There are many workshops for improving relationships. People sign up for them everyday. The only problem is that they are all based on the same hedonistic and self-centered paradigm.

When a male takes on a mission to improve the quality of life for others and powerfully funds it, this becomes the rite of passage into manhood. My wife and other women tell me this is what they want in a man. Women want men to be powerful partners in taking care of *all* human beings, not just themselves and their families.

But many women keep their "boys" the way they are. Women as well as men are focused on getting "things": jewelry, clothes, vacations, fine homes and cars. When they're trying to get men to give them these things, they use sex as an inducement. In this way women reinforce the system that has them end up with a boy instead of a man. He may be a big boy, he may be a good-looking boy, but he is still a boy.

I've spent countless hours in seminars and workshops, starting with Dale Carnegie in the '60's, through nearly every program offered by Werner Erhard into the '90's. Along the way I've taken workshops with Arnold Siegel, Fernando Flores, Robert Pante, Joan Geller, Justin Sterling, Bert Dreyfus, Umberto Maturana, Ronald Heifetz, and many others. How many times, in some workshop or another, have I heard some woman say that she was now ready for a "committed relationship" with a man.

To me their communications sound like, "It's time for a husband to take care of me, time to move on from my father's care." Let them say, "I'm ready to empower some man to be great, to support him in delivering on his vision." Watch the heads turn.

All people are empowered when a woman says, with authenticity, "My cup is full; I'm here to empower another." It's a declaration of emancipation.

If you are a woman, I say that to have a stunning relationship you need to claim your money. Then you can work with him to fund whatever is important to both of you, and fund it powerfully. If he's not willing, fund it powerfully yourself. Give as much money as it takes to get the creative juices flowing.

If you're willing to intrude on his complacency, you can help him do what he's never done. He can create money by providing a true service for others, and he can do this without sacrificing.

My wife and I work side by side on our projects. She's editing this book, for example. She doesn't allow me to become too comfortable. She continually challenges my ingenuity in our drive to fund the end of hunger. It's a circus! We keep discovering more ways in which to serve people and we get paid for providing the service. Though in one sense our life is invented newly day by day, there is wholeness and a flow to it. It is directed by our commitment to catalyze the world's resources towards ending hunger on the planet on the way to society-wide transformation.

At this juncture I want to remind you of what I said in the Preface. This book is not a "how to" guide. It won't tell you how to get rich quick, it won't tell you how to have multiple orgasms. This book is designed to provide a new context in which to hold money, sex, and everything else.

The subject of sex is highly charged with negative emotions such as fear, anger, regret, remorse, and jealousy. It's an area in which we're very vulnerable. By sex, I mean the act of sexual intercourse, often-mislabeled lovemaking. Though we speak of sex as an act of intimacy, we all know that one can have sex without intimacy and intimacy without sex. We will suffer from unfulfilled expectations when we confuse sex with intimacy. *Sex* and *sexual intercourse* are defined by Webster as, "anything having to do with sexual gratification or reproduction." Notice that Webster doesn't include intimacy or lovemaking in this definition. He defines *intimate* as "most private or personal, pertaining to the innermost character of a thing," or, as a verb, "to make known."

Perhaps a qualification for becoming truly intimate is letting another into your life, allowing yourself to be known, making yourself vulnerable.

The problem is, if we allow ourselves to be known, we'll be found out as the jerks, failures, and weirdos we are. If we make ourselves vulnerable we'll be hurt and rejected, perhaps damaged irrevocably. Paradoxically, we get married to avoid being alone, and then in our relationships we avoid being intimate!

There's only one area that I've found to be as fraught with anxiety, self-doubt, and upset as sex, and that's money. In my years of speaking with hundreds of people about money, as their financial planner and their insurance agent and as a fundraiser, I've seen an even greater avoidance of intimacy, of revealing ourselves, in the area of our financial practices than in the area of our sex lives.

There's something like a taboo against asking even those close to you (maybe *particularly* those close to you!) -- your father, say, or your lover -- how much money they make.
Nora, the waitress in the movie "White Palace", says to her lover, Max: "You sleep with me, you're inside of me, and you won't even tell me how much f------ rent you pay!"

As I said before, money is the subject that precipitates the greatest number of marital arguments. Sex is second. A boy's greatest fantasies are of getting rich and getting laid. Particularly with money, the paradox is clear. With one breath we say money is the solution to all our problems. In the next breath we say money is the root of all evil.

All this began to clear up for me in when I took a stand that I create money, that there's no scarcity of money, and that I use money to invest in a better world. Likewise I took the stand that I create ecstasy, that there is no scarcity of ecstasy, and that I use ecstasy to invest in the intimacy of my relationships. I say that ecstasy and intimacy are functions of intention.

ALIVENESS

I'm suggesting a new currency -- one that measures how alive you are. Don't show me your bank account; I can see in your eyes if you're rich. I can see it in your body posture. When you get your attention off yourself, when you start sharing yourself, it shows.

Aliveness is like being lucky. Your feet don't seem to touch the ground. You feel magical. Your juices are flowing. That's how it is when your life is about having others make it instead of worrying about filling your own cup. That's how it is when *you* determine how your day will be, not your boss or the weather.

Helen Keller said: "Security is mostly a superstition. It does not exist in nature, nor do the children of men as a whole experience it. Avoiding danger is no safer in the long run than outright exposure. Life is either a daring adventure or nothing."

Take on something "beyond you" and you'll find yourself capable of reaching beyond what you thought were your limits. Most of us live pretty carefully controlled lives -- lives designed to keep us well within our comfort zone.

PEACE OF MIND

When you are serving others you are at peace with yourself. You're not worried about how others see you, you're just interested in getting the job done. You've made it as a human being -- you can stop trying to get there. You can "go for it" without being concerned if you did it right. You can examine what you did at the end of the day, to see if it worked to serve others, and you can put in corrections for tomorrow.

I see my job as making this world a better place for everyone in it. Having this purpose shuts off the little voice in the back of my head that is always cautioning me to play safe, be careful, hold back. In the past I listened to that little voice's instructions, and I produced little results. When you create a big game for yourself you call upon every known resource.

I keep reminding myself: THERE'S LOTS OF MONEY. IT SHOWS UP WHEN IT'S NEEDED!

When you get in over your head, when you take on a big enough commitment, there's no room for addictions -- whether drugs or booze or food -- and no room for looking good in the eyes of others. When you find yourself being used by your commitments, by a purpose larger than your own personal concerns, you'll find contentment greater than any you've ever known.

The way to really control your life is by giving up your need for control. It's the only way. When you take the attention off yourself, you can get down to some real work. Put a different way, when you stop running after contentment, contentment can overtake you.

JOY

When you don't need anything for yourself, joy is possible. You can really let loose, can laugh at yourself in a healthy, non-deprecating way. You can dance and sing without concern about how you look.

Joy comes from not being attached. It's true freedom. If you knew you were going to die and could accept it, you would be a great person to be around. A person that has accepted his/her own death is not attached to anything. When one operates out of needing something, some form of survival enters in. No joy.

We have turned money into something with human properties. Otherwise we wouldn't be so attached to it. Notice that we are not personally attached to trees. There's the tree over there, separate from us standing over here. We may like the tree, we may call it our tree, but we can leave and the tree stays. We're very clear that we are people and trees are trees. Money occurs for most of us as a part of us, a necessary part. We can't part from it without getting something comparable in return -- that's attachment.

People can't be separated from their money without experiencing anxiety, nervousness, and a sense of loss. We've made up that it's part of us, even that we *are* our money. I've written in an earlier chapter about people who committed suicide when they lost their money, as if their money was their very being.

This attachment to money was clearly demonstrated at a fundraising training for European Hunger Project volunteers that I helped to facilitate several years ago. Sixty men and women of all ages from ten different countries came for this training to Munich, Germany. During the session I was leading I asked them to sit in a circle of chairs facing outward. I stood in the center of the circle talking to the backs of their heads. I asked the participants to take a piece of currency out of their wallets and examine it.

They studied their German marks, French francs, Swiss francs, British pounds, Swedish kroner, and so on. I then instructed them to pass this piece of currency to the person on their right. Even before the game began there were protests. I would ask them to pass money until I said stop, then I would ask them to share what was going on. Very few people were into my game. Hardly anyone was smiling. They were -- upset!

"I can't see my money." "What will happen to our money?" They were going nuts. Some people *wouldn't* pass the money. Others, typically people who acknowledged that they never seemed to have money in their lives, had no money when I stopped the game.

At one point, I had an assistant stand at one end of the oval and hold onto all the money as it came to her. Soon she had collected all the money. I said that the game was over and joked that this was the new way of raising money for The Hunger Project. Then I asked the participants to share what this experience was like for them. One woman started laughing. When I asked why, she said that she had borrowed the money, so it didn't matter. The friend from whom she'd borrowed was angry when it became evident that the borrower didn't feel responsible for paying her back.

Some people were outraged when I said with a straight face, "Thanks for your contribution to The Hunger Project." They said, "This is a trick! We can't trust The Hunger Project." A whole range of human emotions was present, but noticeably absent was joy. We then gave them back all their money. Our point was to demonstrate to these potential fundraisers just how crazed people are about their money. A fundraiser had better know that before asking for big contributions. It's delicate territory.

After a break, we conducted a real contribution meeting where we offered the participants the opportunity to fund The Hunger Project. They responded by pledging more money than they ever imagined they could give. The conference was very joyful from that point on. People had gotten freedom from their attachment to money. And we saw the resulting partnership of the different Hunger Project affiliates in Europe as a harbinger of the partnership of European nations.

In the years since then, our European volunteers have become leaders at contributing money to and raising money for The Hunger Project of Europe, rather than The Hunger Projects of France, Switzerland, Germany, Belgium, and so forth. Since that time the Berlin Wall has come down, the European Economic Community is becoming a reality, and the people of Eastern Europe have taken a stand for freedom and democracy.

When I look back on my years of involvement with The Hunger Project, it seems like a series of joyful events all blended together, with a few distinctive highlights. One of these memories is of participating with my friend and fellow fundraiser, the late actor Raul Julia. Lee and I met Raul and his lovely wife Merel at a Hunger Project contribution meeting that I was co-leading in 1984. The Julias have been committed to The Hunger Project since its inception in 1977. Raul shared with us at the meeting that he was temporarily out of work and that he was borrowing money from his agent to support his family.

We asked him, and the others in the room, "What amount of money, if you gave it, would be an authentic expression of your personal commitment to ending hunger?" The participants agonized for a while. Some gave a lot, some a little, some nothing.

Raul and Merel pledged $15,000 for the year that night. It knocked us out. They had said when invited, "We'll come because we love The Hunger Project, but we're pretty sure we can't give any money." At the meeting they found themselves unwilling to be stopped by their existing circumstances. They did fulfill the pledge. Raul went on to host similar meetings to which he invited his friends -- actors, actresses, producers and others involved in the theater. From that point on until his death in 1994, Raul was working steadily on stage and in films -- and working brilliantly. He would sometimes call me from backstage between acts, to update me on his Hunger Project results and to get coaching.

He and Merel invested increasingly larger amounts of money in The Hunger Project; the largest was $250,000 in one year. They were on our steering committee and Raul at a meeting meant fun. He was outrageous. He sang louder than anyone at our dinners. He was constantly on TV sharing his commitment and encouraging others to join in. Many big name stars looked up to Raul and Merel. Their relationship was a vital and loving one, and it was a joy to be with them.

Joy is natural to human beings. When we take off our heavy armor we can swing out. We can get a sense of this by being with little kids, by listening to their laughter, by seeing the light shining in their eyes. How bright and fresh and unlimited they are! Let the little kid inside you back into your life.

POWER WITH MONEY

The power to give money cannot be accessed when we have attachments or needs. Whatever we're attached to will override any vision of contribution and bring us back to our attachments and needs with a snap like that of a rubber band.

Let's review the definition of paradigm: "A set of rules and regulations that 1) describes boundaries; and 2) tells you what to do to be successful within those boundaries."

A paradigm tells you what the game is and how to play it successfully. In the current money game, we are told: "Accumulate wealth, invest it, and live off the interest. Don't touch the principal; build your pile." Those who do this have played the game successfully. No wonder money is stuck, and it is difficult to get it flowing.

Being attached is literally like having one foot nailed to the floor. One reason it's hard to move out of one paradigm into another is that we're just as attached to the rules we've made as we are to the money we've made. Another reason it's hard is that we don't *know* we're attached. We protest that we're free and we give evidence like, "I take off work whenever I want and I give lots of money to charity." Even when we acknowledge that we feel trapped we don't see that we're trapped by our attachments. We think we're trapped by circumstances and that those circumstances are inevitable.

Generally speaking, human beings hate change. We'll sometimes put up with truly painful conditions simply because they're familiar. The way it is, the status quo, becomes our security blanket. And often we don't see any alternative anyway. We are so dominated by money that we see no real possibility of directing it with freedom and power. This is because we see money as scarce.

As you can imagine, I deliberately bring into my conversations with friends, clients and colleagues the possibility of freedom from money -- and I explore how that might look in the life of the person with whom I'm speaking. One woman gave as evidence she was not attached to money that she spent a lot of money on clothes. She felt that buying things was a way of circulating money. What she was actually doing was exchanging money for things, expecting to get value in the exchange.

People who contribute to their favorite charities may be deceiving themselves into thinking, like my clothes-buying friend, that they too are moving money. But most often charitable giving is done out of the present paradigm, contribution as sacrifice -- whether with hope or without hope that it will do any good. We give up some of our pile to help those who are not as well off as we are. And we know they never will be as well off, because the amount of money in the world is finite and the way it's distributed is fixed. While we may feel that it is our obligation to help others, making sure we have more than enough for ourselves is paramount.

When you see money as an instrument of change, even of transformation, your worldview can shift. I now see that the hungry people are not helpless, hapless victims but human beings with the same desire to live lives of dignity, meaning and contribution that we have. When we see that money is needed as an investment in the sustainable future of humanity we supply it, with no sense of sacrifice. Then we go get more from the unlimited supply in the universe.

Shifting our point of view about money will have a powerful impact on all other domains. For example, if we could see money as unlimited, we would be on our way towards ending prejudice in the world. We wouldn't see people who are different from us as a threat. We'd be free to relate to people as our family, as our partners in universal productivity, as our team.

I've seen that I've created all the money I've ever had by either earning, winning, borrowing, or receiving it as a gift. More important, I've also seen that I have the power to direct it. For the last twenty years I have been directing hundreds of thousands of dollars into The Hunger Project so that we can have a world without hunger.

My wife and I have told The Hunger Project that we are committed to making pledges that seem impossible to fulfill. We can be counted on to continually use our money pledges to expand our ability to produce what's needed to end hunger by the end of the century. When we make the amount high enough and the time frame short enough so that we're stretched, sometimes even a little crazed, we know we're creating a condition from which new and unexpected resources can be called. This is how we empower ourselves with money, and we share this empowerment with the intention of empowering others. We may not always fulfill our pledges, but who we've become in the process is powerful, and in the end, we believe, an invincible force!

The other arena in which I have an opportunity to support people in being powerful with money is in my business. The Traband Associates, which I founded, has been filling the insurance needs of professionals and business owners for about 40 years. We started selling insurance in southern New Jersey and we now have clients all over the country. For most of our history we specialized in life insurance products. In 1986 we realized that most of our clients were lacking the foundation of disability insurance to deal with long term illness or injury.

Our commitment was to have our clients covered by disability insurance with the maximum payout and the minimum exceptions, in other words, an optimal policy we call AIRTIGHT COMPREHENSIVE DISABILITY INSURANCE. I say that our optimal disability insurance became available as a distinction out of our stand for ourselves as optimal human beings -- as champions for all people making it. I suggest that from this kind of stand you can create anything -- money, resources, time, energy -- and that you can then direct them towards your commitments in highly leveraged ways. You become a director of global resources when you're a "part owner of the planet." You can even direct future resources (e.g., when the mortgage is paid off or the kids graduate from college) into a current commitment. Declaring oneself an optimal human being, and out of that declaration becoming responsible for one's power and resourcefulness, begins the inquiry into what practices are consistent with this role.

Brian Regnier, an executive of Landmark Education in San Francisco, started the Caregivers Project in the early 90's. This project was designed to take care of people who take care of others, particularly the terminally ill. He noticed that caregivers who don't listen to warning signals often burn themselves out. This can be a problem for others as well as for themselves. As George Bernard Shaw writes in *Man and Superman*:

> "Self-sacrifice enables us to sacrifice other people without blushing. If you begin by sacrificing yourself to those you love, you will end by hating those to whom you have sacrificed yourself."

Prior to 1986, although I was selling disability insurance to my customers, I had no disability insurance myself. I assumed "it couldn't happen to me" even though I was exposed to all the insurance literature, charts, and tables, as well as the actual claims of my customers and friends. One day, a friend of mine at the home office of an insurance company with which I was doing business, asked me what kind of disability income protection I owned. He was shocked to hear that I had dropped my disability insurance a few years earlier. He asked me what plan I had for supporting myself in the event of a disability. After trying to convince him that no illness or injury could stop me from selling insurance, I finally saw that I had no firm foundation for my financial future. All I had was a hope that in the remote event that I'd suffer a disability, my insurance customers would stay with me and I would live off of their renewals. I was kidding myself.

I'm thankful that he stuck with me until I woke up. Now I have a foolproof disability insurance plan that will back up my commitment to always pay my own way. What I saw was that my reasons for not having insurance stemmed from my unwillingness to pay for it. Once again I uncovered that old bugaboo, scarcity. My practices of "either-or" were undermining my context of sufficiency. By taking the stand that I am sufficient, and having my practices be consistent with that stand, I began to produce greater and greater business results. I say it's no accident that my wife and I can take time to volunteer for The Hunger Project, take many great vacations, and take on new projects -- all this without sacrificing our business results.

Once I became responsible for my life and my finances, I was free to produce.

I can't emphasize this enough. What do I mean -- free to produce? Producing is normally associated with working; and we usually see work as something we do to survive and get ahead, not as a freedom. When I declared that I was sufficient to handle anything that came along and took actions consistent with this declaration, such as purchasing optimal disability insurance, my point of view about work and producing changed. I saw work, producing results and contributing to others, as a privilege.

I'm also grateful to my friend for sticking with me until I saw the need to protect my income. It has been a line of demarcation in my life. By opening up this conversation for getting my house of protection in order, he woke me up to my own scarcity thinking. If being disabled means being unable to respond, then isn't a person who is resisting spending money on something of value somewhat weakened and susceptible to other calamities? I ask my prospective clients to think of themselves as the internal purchasing agent for the disabled person they could become, to take responsibility for protecting that person's future.

About 15 years ago I participated with one hundred other people in a weeklong course that involved some scary exercises on high cliffs. We were reassured that everything was totally safe. There were backup safety lines, nets, and harnesses. I was free to experience exhilaration, mastery, and full self-expression because the "insurance" was in place to guarantee my safety.

My wife, Lee, suggested that we hire a consultant to coach us on contributing greater and greater amounts of money to The Hunger Project. We have many management consultants as insurance clients and friends. We interviewed a number of them to see if they would commit to working with us on our project to generate enough money for us to continue our lifestyle *and* invest hundreds of thousands of dollars in our commitment to end hunger.

We decided upon a business consultant who typically charges hundreds of dollars an hour for working with companies like Eastman Kodak and Mobil. He agreed to be our coach in this project and immediately started requesting information on our cash flow, debts, and assets.

We were expecting to pay him at least $1,000 a month and we had agreed that whatever he charged would be worth it. We were shocked when he said; "I'm not charging you for this. I'll be just as thrilled as you if you continually invest substantial money in such a valuable program for humanity." We couldn't believe that we had one of the most effective people in America on our side, available to keep us focused. We are ensuring fulfillment without sacrifice.

What does it mean to have it all? Another more telling question is, are we willing to pay the price for having it all? If we're not, we'll continue to embrace mediocrity. If we're committed to being free from money, we need to put our money where our hearts are. Don't expect discounts or free rides -- they only come to those who don't need them. Because we are committed to being "free from money" in a way that permits us to be "free with money," miracles are occurring for us. We don't *expect* discounts or free rides, but somehow, and I suspect it's because we don't *need* them, we're getting a full measure of those too. And so can you.

CHAPTER 7

HOW TO CREATE IT THE WAY YOU WANT IT

"An unlived life is not worth examining."
                                                    - Jane Bonin

A few years ago I saw the movie, *Gandhi*. This man designed his life around taking stands -- both in his native India and in South Africa. He lived his life as a statement that he was a resource for every person, whatever their color, whatever their religion, whatever their station or condition.

Rather than limiting his loyalty to India, he invented himself as a global citizen.

"I am a human being," he said. "That's the parade I will march in." And I said, "Me too, Mahatma!" Joining forces with Gandhi is a good first step towards freeing oneself from the addiction of money.

There are critical distinctions within stand taking. For example, certain individuals are granted the authority to declare people married, by the state and the religious institution. Others are authorized to call a baseball pitch a ball or a strike. They are called umpires. The way you and I can take a stand is not based on official authorization and it's very powerful. Like Gandhi, we can say who we are in the matter of our future. We can declare our purpose, our commitments, what others can count on us for. In fact, we can create something that may not have existed before. The baseball umpire calls the pitch a ball or a strike. Before his call, it wasn't a ball or a strike; it was just a pitch. He doesn't have to prove it. No one gets to overturn his call. His word is final.

The preacher calls two people husband and wife, and before she said the words, they were just two people who wanted to get married.

When we take a stand we are setting up the way it will be simply by saying so. Only human beings have that ability. When we take a stand we no longer operate in the same reality. We are no longer bound by the same opinions and beliefs. Taking a stand breaks the hold addiction has on us.

By taking a stand we can design our life on our terms. We can write the script. And we can interpret our lives in terms of the stands we have taken. We can say that money is to be used in the service of everyone. We can say that we are sufficient, that we have enough.

That doesn't mean that you won't get more; it means that you don't *need* more. It means you'd be fine if you didn't accumulate more money. It means that your stand for being sufficient is senior to your circumstances and your addictions. It grants you the ability to create the future out of your speaking.

When it looks like I am over my head in some project and my wife asks how she can support me, I tell her to relate to me as if I am Houdini. When I don't see any way to my goal, I count on Lee to say to me, "Houdini, here's a situation tailor-made for you. This looks impossible. Go for it." This helps me remember that I have resources I've not tapped. A new person -- Houdini -- shows up to handle the dragons.

A key to this Houdini deal is that she never says, "OK, Houdini, how are you going to get out of *this* mess?" She co-creates the context that I am unstoppable; she puts me in touch with my resources so that I can be in action instead of paralyzed. She calls me "Tradini!"

DESIGNING AN INVESTMENT BEFORE YOU PUT DOWN YOUR MONEY

In looking at where to invest my money, I have some criteria that you may not have thought of. Here's an obvious one: If I take cocaine, I've been told, I'll feel better than I have ever felt in my life. So why don't I buy it? Sounds like a good deal. Wouldn't this be a better investment than many other things? Lots of other people are investing in crack; shouldn't I follow the crowd?

The answer in this case is obvious enough. I could end up in jail, and I don't want that. I could end up addicted, and I don't want that. I could lose my reputation and my credibility, and I don't want that. I could lose my life, and I sure don't want that. So cocaine doesn't look like a good investment to me; it looks like a con.

And here's another one: What about a great car? I've always had great cars. Over the last twenty years I've owned a Mercedes, a Lincoln, a vintage Bentley, and three BMW's. My last car was a Jaguar XJS. The Jag got me lots of attention. Everybody thought I was cool. People were always asking me about my Jag. Sounds like a good investment.

But there's another side to this -- more information, so to speak. The 48-month lease was $778 per month. The insurance was very high. I felt obliged to keep it spotless. It's not an easy car to get a body in and out of. The cost of repairs and accessories was off the charts -- all Jaguar owners have horror stories to tell about time and money spent in the shop. Good investment? It had downsides as well as upsides.

Isn't real estate a good investment? Like anything, it is when it is and its not when it's not. Right now people are saying it is not a good investment. What about stocks and mutual funds ... oil wells ... paintings ... annuities? What are the "for sure" characteristics of a great investment? When I'm looking for a great investment, I want to be sure that it doesn't lead to addiction, something like cocaine, because addiction means loss of control, sometimes, even loss of life.

Anne Wilson Schaef puts the case trenchantly in her book, *When Society Becomes An Addict*:

> "In our culture the process of accumulating money often becomes addictive. Like any other addiction it is progressive; it takes more and more to achieve a fix, and eventually no amount is enough." And she goes on to say, "Often they do not care about money in and of itself; what drives them is the series of actions and interactions involved in accumulating it."

Let's look at inheritance in this context. Consider the possibility that people with inherited wealth are being saddled with the previous generation's addictions, rather like being a crack baby. Oftentimes wealthy people begin to make distributions while they're still alive, usually with strings attached. Either explicitly or implicitly this message comes through -- "The money is to be held in trust; do not spend the principal!"

The *real* return on an investment can best be measured by what you're left with. Are you left with more love for people and from people, more appreciation and a deeper connection with the human family? Do you have more energy? Do you have more trust in your ability to deal with difficulties on your own? Are you more open to being contributed to? Are you more easily moved? Are you left more powerful, more able to stand on your own two feet, more independent and resourceful?

Does this investment get you out on the floor to dance and sing? Does your word have more power? Are you operating with more integrity? Are you free of medications and alcohol and cigarettes? Are you more aware of the world around you? Do you wake up alive and refreshed?

Have you a vision for the world? Did this investment help create a cleaner, more healthy environment? Did it forward your commitment to the end of hunger, the end of prejudice, the end of the subjugation of women and the end of war? Will your children -- will *all* our children -- have a brighter future as a result of this investment?

Have you ever heard of an investment that could produce such results? Wouldn't it be ideal? Most investments have a downside. Is it possible to have at least one investment that is a complete win for everyone? Can we experience well being through serving humanity *and* still make a "killer" profit? Which looks like the better investment -- one that produces an annual monetary return of 20%, or one that produces all the above benefits?

One example of a "can't miss" high-return investment for me and for many of my friends continues to be The Hunger Project. No doubt there are other programs and projects that fit this description, but for the past twenty years I've been paying close attention to the returns on my Hunger Project investment, and I haven't seen a better deal anywhere. If and when I do find something better, I'll be sure to put my money there.

Year after year my wife and I give far more money to The Hunger Project than our accountant and tax attorney want us to give. They caution us every year. Even our friends and family sometimes worry that we will end up in the poorhouse. But out of our stand that we are sufficient we have become masterful with our money and our lives are unbelievable. We are doing what we want to do, indeed what we love to do, day in and day out. Being of service to our insurance clients is as much a joy as a job for us, and this is because we operate out of appreciation for people's commitments rather than out of apprehension over people's addictions.

Lee and I work side by side in our business, side by side in our volunteer work for the end of hunger, and side by side in our house. We're together nearly twenty-four hours a day, and we truly enjoy each other. We have the love, trust, and respect of our family and hundreds of friends. We look ten to twenty years younger than our ages. We are convinced that the main thing we have going for us is that we say we have enough. We don't need any of what you've got. We don't need what the next guy's got. And we don't just talk this way; we live this way -- in such a complete sense of sufficiency that our experience is one of plenitude, of bounty and largesse. That is the feedback we get from those who know us.

CHAPTER 8

STEP ONE: AUTHORIZING YOURSELF TO TAKE A STAND

The purpose of this chapter is to lay the groundwork for you to alter your future. It's to let you know that you have a certain power, the power to take a stand. Chances are you have never before taken a stand in the creative and empowering sense I am proposing. There is a technology available for taking a stand that can produce a transformation in your relationship with money -- and with other things in your life as well.

Once you commit yourself to creating your own sufficiency -- and begin to work within this commitment -- opportunities open up for you on every hand. The work is somewhat like learning a foreign language; when you dedicate yourself to it, ever expanding dimensions of another culture become available to you. And though it takes a lot of work in the beginning, the learning gets easier and goes faster over time. The payoff from learning this new "money language" is control over all the financial aspects of your life, no matter how much or how little money you have. This work begins by learning the distinction "taking a stand," then practicing it as you would practice declensions and conjugations in a foreign language.

When you take a stand for a future to which you're committed, a future radically different from the past, you are doing what those who made history did. Gandhi took a stand, Martin Luther King, Jr. took a stand, Abraham Lincoln took a stand. Taking a stand is not a prerogative reserved for world leaders only. You and I can take a stand as well.

We take stands by speaking, by inventing a future for ourselves. For example, we can say that what we spend money on empowers us, makes us stronger, more able to prosper, more able to be of service. When we speak our future, we are laying new track in front of us, charting a course in previously uncharted waters.

And the action of speaking our future can alter our lives in the present as well. When we start behaving in a manner consistent with the future we have designed, our ineffective complaining yields to effective planning, and our under-the-breath grumbling gives way to the making of clear requests. Things that were stuck start to move, not by the employment of force, but through the conscious and creative development of our intentions.

I have found that standing for my values and purposes and goals in the future gives me a present full of joy and freedom. I wake up in the morning eager to discover ways to make my clients' and my friends' and my family's lives more joyous and fulfilling. I've changed my orientation from wanting to get, to wanting to give, from being needful for myself to being useful for others.

A NEW TECHNOLOGY: TAKING A STAND

This technology was made available to me through courses and seminars designed by Landmark Education. What follows is my interpretation of the principles of taking a stand, and my formula for applying these principles to everyday living. The application of these principles has produced miracles in my life; and I pass this technology on to you with the intention that you produce miracles in your life.

Before defining what I mean by a stand, it may be useful to say what a stand is *not*. It is not, for example, an opinion. People have opinions about everything under the sun. Have you ever noticed that dinner party conversations are almost entirely opinion, and that no matter how eloquently they are presented, they don't make any difference in people's lives? Neither is a stand a truth that can be proved with evidence, like the earth is round. It's been useful for me to make distinctions between facts, my own opinions and stands -- useful to see that what makes a difference is when I speak what I stand for.

Another way of saying "to take a stand" is "to make a declaration." There are many types of declaration. For example, there are declarations made by people invested with authority, as when a minister pronounces a couple man and wife. If *I* say, "I now pronounce you man and wife," it means nothing. I have no authority to marry people. But if a person possessing proper authority says it, you are married. An umpire has the authority to call pitches either balls or strikes. The umpire's word is final, whether the pitch was inside or outside the strike zone. The jury can declare you guilty whether or not you broke the law.

Another form of declaration is that which is self-authorized, for example, forgiveness. Many people do not realize they can close the book on some long-standing matter just by *saying so*. They think something has to happen, like what's owed being paid them, or an apology being made. A few years ago a friend of mine in the insurance business convinced two of my clients to drop the insurance they had with me and to buy insurance from him. It was my *opinion* that he had used underhanded methods, and that he had honored neither our friendship nor the clients' welfare. For five years I avoided him, and when his name came up in conversation, I spoke ill of him.

Finally, noticing how much energy I was expending in my rejection of him, I called him up and apologized -- for snubbing him and gossiping about him. I took a stand for our friendship rather than for our falling out. He forgave me, and since that day I have been free of the strain of alienation I had been experiencing. I took a stand that I had no more resentment, and I backed it up with action to make my stand real in the world.

This book is about getting free from the domination of money. Declaration is the path to that freedom. You could follow me around for days, listening to all the sound monetary advice I give to people, and never get free from the domination of money. You'd get a lot of good ideas, but without declaring yourself you would never have freedom in the area of money. You may be thinking that certain circumstances have to be in place for you to make this declaration, to take a stand for your sufficiency. For example, you may think you need to have a particular net worth, or a particular position, before you can declare yourself. I say you are free from money when 1) you know what a declaration is; 2) you know that you can make a declaration; 3) you take a stand that you are free from money; and 4) you take actions correlated with this freedom, actions that will make your stand become a reality.

If you are a public speaker, you can take the stand that everything you say contributes to people and that whatever nervousness you have transforms into energy and passion to accomplish your goal. The effectiveness of your talk does not need to be measured by whether your audience agrees with you, because now you are looking to see what you can contribute to them. Your attention is not on how you sound or look but rather on serving your audience. Once you've taken the stand that *you* are a contribution, then that includes your clothes, your speech, your stutter, your nervousness, everything.

You will be using a particular kind of feedback to forward and fine-tune your contribution. You will ask yourself whether your audience was moved. Did people stay afterwards to talk to you? Did they lighten up? Did anyone take a stand? You will ask how *you* were left at the end of your talk.

In the old paradigm of public speaking, you might hope for people to came up and say, "You were wonderful; I could never do anything like that." In the new paradigm you will be looking for responses like, "I will take action; I am altered." So you know that they will be sharing their new future with others, that your work will be going on through them. When you contribute to people in this way, you've given them your power and your energy. You've shared it all, not just given them crumbs from your plate. And the more you share it, the more you have available to you.

When we look at money within this new paradigm, we see that it could end crime, prejudice, hunger, and war. When a critical mass of people relates to money as a resource in a public sense -- instead of something to which we feel personally entitled -- I say the world will flip over, sunny-side up!

Wayne Dyer, the motivational speaker and writer, has wrote a novel called *Gifts from Eykis*, in which a person from another planet visits earth. She is shocked at how *attached* we are to money. Seeing myself and my fellow humans through her alien eyes has proved to be both amusing and enlightening. His book drives home the point that, generally speaking, it is much more accurate to say, "money has us" than that "we have money"!

Many of our practices reveal that we are addicted to money, but given the stigma associated with addiction, it may be a painful and difficult thing to admit. But unless you notice and intervene in these addictive practices, this book will be just information -- and information without action doesn't make a difference. People who are overweight *know* they should not eat so much, but having that knowledge does not alter their condition. Most smokers *know* that smoking is harmful to their health, but having that knowledge does not keep them from smoking. Look at other addictions and you will see the same pattern. In this book you will learn how to practice breaking the hold addictions have on you. We can continue to live out of our wants and desires, our habitual "cravings," or we can begin living our lives according to our stand.

Living according to our stand -- "living as our word" -- means calling the way it's going to go *before the game*, then playing the game out of that call. It means interpreting money as a resource for fulfillment -- because that's what we say it is -- and then finding appropriate places to use that resource. Once we find places to employ money, rather than merely spending it, we become inspired to become creative in attracting the money needed for the jobs at hand.

To take a stand one doesn't need to stand *on* anything; one simply takes the stand. There need be no justification for the stand, no argument, no validation. There are no prerequisites. To take a stand is an act of venturing, an act of courage. An authentic stand lives in the universe as "a clearing" (attitude, climate, environment) for what's being stood for. That clearing allows, in fact brings forth, those interpretations and those actions which are consistent with the stand. It does so naturally, not as a forced resolution. Indeed, neither resolutions nor convictions nor ideals are necessary to create the clearing for taking an authentic stand.

Taking a stand is an action any individual can take, and in that action they join all others who have taken that stand. This is very important. When a human being takes a stand, he/she becomes part of a universal conversation which can bring into being a new paradigm. For example, when we take a stand for freedom and equal opportunity for all, we become part of the body of people who have lived their lives out of that stand, no matter when they lived. We join ranks with Martin Luther King, Rosa Parks and Gandhi, transcending time and transforming history.

CONCLUSION

You are able to alter your future by taking a stand and taking actions consistent with your stand. You can totally get out of this money trap that blunts your power and your self-expression by creating a new context around the issue of money. You now know the definition of a stand, and you know that you have the power to take a stand. This is the key to freedom from suffering. This is the key to taking your life into your own hands.

The next chapter points to the specific stand you will want to take when you are ready to grant yourself freedom from the constraints money places on you. Subsequent chapters will suggest actions that will make your new stand real and make it available to others around you that you care about. Get out your highlighter, pen, and paper -- the work of emancipation begins!

CHAPTER 9

IT'S ALL IN THE SET-UP

"Give me a place to stand and I will move the earth."
- Archimedes

Now that you know the key elements of taking a stand, you need no longer be dominated by the need for money and possessions -- either by what you have or what you don't have. You can now authentically declare that you are sufficient, resourceful, up to any challenge - regardless of your personal circumstances. When this declaration settles deep in your bones you will automatically take powerful actions with money.

By taking the stand that you are sufficient you will begin to alter your life. When you look at the problems and issues in front of you as a sufficient person rather than a person in scarcity, you will find yourself handling those situations which up until now have been dominating you.

Everything that we value has come out of human beings taking stands: for example, the right to life, liberty and the pursuit of happiness, for which our forefathers took a stand in 1776. Out of this stand, a new future for humanity was created -- all over the world people were aroused and stimulated by possibilities heretofore unknown to them.

This chapter is about building a solid foundation beneath your stand. If your foundation has cracks in it, the structure you build on it won't stand up against adversity. The more work you put into laying a solid base, the greater the possibility for a lasting structure.

I now have the power to continually invent my life; I no longer merely extend my past. It's like jumping over my own shadow. The more I accomplish, the more I'm interested in breaking apart the limits and restrictions of my life. I've learned to leapfrog my accomplishments rather than rest on my laurels.

We've all seen this phenomenon of taking a stand in movies and books. There appear to be no prerequisites. It doesn't seem to matter if you are in shape or out of shape, or if you do or don't have money. Higher education is not required. You don't have to have a job or a spouse. Your bills don't have to be current. In other words, taking a stand is not part of a package or a sequence. It operates outside of linear time.

In the movie *The Big Easy*, a New Orleans police detective on the take turns his life around and gets integrity with the help of his girlfriend. Overnight, he becomes a new person. How does he do this? How could we?

Okay. It's a movie, and we live in the real world where "rocks are hard and water is wet." Suppose the economy has been bad. Everybody knows you have to be conservative in such times. But the truth is you can take a stand at any time -- just like in the movies.

When we change our focus, when we shift the paradigm in which we've been operating by taking a stand, it's like changing the force field of our personal magnet. People who are at the same level of integrity are attracted to us. Those who haven't made the shift may not be speaking our language, the language of possibility, but we need not see them as hostile. When you start seeing money and possessions as a means to serve all others, rather than as something you need, then money and possessions don't hook you anymore.

MONEY AS THE ANSWER, THE CURE-ALL

We've been told that money solves all problems, that if we have a lot of money we can buy whatever we want. We've been told over and over that having money will satisfy us. Yet we're still trapped. We're still run by money.

Here's a short scenario from one of Larry McMurtry's novels, *Some Can Whistle*. The main character of the book is enormously wealthy. He lives in a fabulous house in Texas, in the hills, far from the nearest town. He's in his early fifties, has made hundreds of millions in television, and now wants to be left alone. He has a $60,000 Mercedes that he hasn't driven in six months. One day he needs to drive into town and it won't start. He finally realizes that he's going to have to call a local garage to come get the car started. He feels helpless and ordinary.

Here are this character's thoughts as set down in McMurtry's book:

> "In the particular world in which I became successful -- the world of entertainment, or, to be more precise, the world of television -- no illusion is more crucial than the illusion that great success and huge money buy you immunity from the common ills of mankind, such as cars that won't start. The maxim, the Golden Rule, the first motto of the world in which I achieved my success is: All Things Are Supposed to Work Instantly. If they don't, then what's it all for? The fact that you might have to wait ten minutes to get your car jump-started, like any ordinary slob, calls a whole value system into question. If you don't have total immunity, then why bother?"

You and I can have a lot of money, like the character in McMurtry's book, but we're still part of the ordinary world. The only real difference is that now we've got a lot more money. If we drink too much our heads will still hurt the next day. If we eat too much, we'll still get fat. A good night's sleep comes to rich or poor people. A person who lacks aliveness -- lacks joy, self-expression, a zest for life -- can't buy this with money.

WHO I AM IS RESOURCEFUL BECAUSE I SAY SO AND FOR AS LONG AS I SAY SO.

Create your own stand and it will alter your life whether you ever have a lot of money or not. The suffering will stop. Some of you may still be wondering if you really should be *using* money as opposed to accumulating and preserving it. All you need ask yourself is: "Is my life joyful? Am I thrilled when the electric bill arrives? Does it give me a high to be asked to contribute a lot of money to charity? Are these negative or positive experiences? Am I free from -- and free with! -- my money?"

This chapter is for people who have committed to becoming paradigm pioneers in the matter of money. Taking a stand is the same as creating a context. If you create a context that you are sufficient, the world will look very different to you: same habits, same circumstances, same bills, but a completely transformed relationship to everything. Problems get ground up in the blender of a new context. For example, create the context that the state police work for you, then, notice how differently they appear to you when you see them on the freeway.

HAVE YOUR DAILY PRACTICES EMPOWER YOU

Even if you pay all your taxes, you probably have done so as an obligation rather than as a privilege. Try creating the interpretation *overjoyed* as you pay your taxes. It works, as I can testify. About fifteen years ago I did exactly that. For years I had hated paying taxes, had hated filling out the forms, had hated talking to my accountant. I remember telling my bookkeeper one day that I was going to stop hating taxes. He was shocked. "Lester," he said, "do you know what you're doing? Everybody hates paying taxes!" I told him I was not falling in love with taxes, just moving up to tolerating them.

For a number of years after this I had to consciously re-enroll myself, particularly when I was audited for a period of three out of four years in the 1980's. I continued to speak "righteously" to other people, particularly those who told me they were getting away with paying little or no taxes, but I was feeling secretly burdened by -- and secretly resentful of paying my full share.

It was then that I saw I needed to take another stand: a stand that I am empowered and enriched by paying my taxes. Why suffer? I was paying my full share; why not get maximum value? Now, because I have declared that paying taxes to my government is a privilege, I feel I can be a full citizen. I can write to elected officials and get results because I'm paying in full, not getting by on the cheap. My accounts with you, the other taxpayers are paid up in full. You're not required to pay higher taxes because I'm paying as little as I can get away with. I'm doing business from a clean slate, it works for me and I'm encouraging you to do the same.

PAYING MY TAXES GIVES ME THE PRIVILEGES OF CITIZENSHIP

Prior to the American Revolution, members of communities would get together once a year to discuss their mutual needs over the next 12 months. Once they agreed to the goods and services required they competed for the right to pay for them. For example, one man would get up and say, "I believe I'm the wealthiest person in this community. I own a number of buildings and four fields; therefore I will pay 12% of the overall expenses." Then another person would stand up and say, "To the contrary, I am the wealthiest. I own three farms and the general store; therefore I will pay 15% of the costs." And so it would go until the required amount of money was raised.

The signers of the Declaration of Independence pledged their lives, their fortunes, and their sacred honor, as naturally they would.   Because these signers came from communities wherein it was an honor to pay one's fair share of expenses.

SERVICE - THE SECRET OF SUCCESS

Mahatma Gandhi almost single-handedly secured the independence of India. He is thought of as superhuman, a saint who had complete control of his life, his habits, his diet, his integrity. It appears that he lived a monastic, sacrificial life. But we must remember that he chose a Spartan course very deliberately and lived like the poorest of the poor with joy and freedom. Where did he get his power? What shifted for him that had him be unstoppable -- not unstoppable like a god or a prophet, but unstoppable as a human being?

It appears that the shift took place early on, when he was a young lawyer in South Africa. It was at this time that he gained power and control over money, and he did this in connection with a certain incident. Interestingly, it was when he gave up money, and his attachment to it, that he became able to use it.

As related by Eknath Easwaran in *Ghandi the Man*, Gandhi was defending a man named Dada Abdne against one of his blood relatives. Gandhi's research showed that the facts backed his client, but Gandhi knew that the legal process could go on for months, and he could see this case driving a deep wedge between the client and his family.

He persuaded both sides to settle out of court. Easwaran observed that Gandhi was ecstatic. " 'I had learned the true practice of law,' Gandhi exclaimed. 'I had learned to find out the better side of human nature and to enter men's hearts. I realized that the true function of a lawyer was to unite parties driven asunder.' "

Easwaren continues:

> "Gandhi, without realizing it, had found THE SECRET OF SUCCESS. [emphasis added] He began to look at

every difficulty and see it as an opportunity for service, a challenge which could draw out of him greater and greater sources of intelligence and imagination. In turning his back on personal profit or prestige in his work, he found he had won the trust and even love of whites and Indians and South Africans alike."

He became very successful overnight. From then on he had power over money. He directed it. Gandhi used it not for war, which is power over others, but to make things work without violence. He moved the world from the context of service, not from the context of profit. He took a non-negotiable stand to serve others.

This whole book could be about Gandhi and his view of money and possessions. For example, it is reported that he balanced his accounts every night, even when he was managing huge amounts of money in the quest for India's independence. On the subject of integrity Gandhi spoke as follows: "One man cannot do right in one department of life whilst he is occupied in doing wrong in any other department. Life is one indivisible whole." He saw no point in giving his children money or paying for their education. He felt that this would have given them the message that they couldn't make it without his financial support. Gandhi took a stand for his own sufficiency and others, and this stand made him virtually unstoppable.

He said he was going to play the game a certain way and then he *walked his talk*. He made it up. He created a context of service. By creating this context he suspended his prejudices and became a global citizen, a whole and complete person. From that moment on he was in control. And in a sense his life became easy, because all he had to do was act consistently with the context he had created for himself.

Do we have to be saints to gain the upper hand with money? Do we have to cut our own way through the jungle? What's wrong with following paths someone else has carved out? If the evidence suggests that those following such paths don't get to their destination, get out your machete and create your own path. But if you notice that they're getting there faster than you, and without any compromise of integrity, then join them!

TELLING YOU WHAT YOU WANT TO HEAR

It is wise to view people who advise you about money and investments with suspicion. The woods are full of those who have you figured out and are saying exactly what "hooks" you. When they hook you, they're into your wallet. When people are offering lots of money in a short period of time, beware.

Financial gurus often lead with statements such as these: "Listen to me, you'll save on taxes.... Become a millionaire with no down payment.... In no time you'll be able to leave your job.... Give me your money and I'll quadruple it in one year." Their courses and tapes have names like: "Wealth Without Risk," "How I Became A Millionaire In My Spare Time," "Money, Wisdom And Wealth." They're successful because they've figured out what people will buy. We are suckers for this stuff. Who doesn't want a big mansion with a Rolls Royce out front, a pool in the back, and a vacation home on the Riviera?

When I was in the U.S. Air Force in the late fifties, stationed in Germany, two of my buddies and I took a great vacation which included the French Riviera. I saw those rich guys riding at anchor on their yachts. I saw the Ferraris and Porsches. They made a big impression on me. At that time it became my personal dream to have a yacht on the French Riviera -- Cannes, St. Tropez, Antibes. In my dream I'd ride at anchor in one of these ports, drinking expensive wine and watching everybody walk by envying me. Maybe I'd have my captain take me for a cruise once in awhile, but the big deal would be how conspicuous I was, how obviously "a winner." Years later my wife would ask, "Why do you always want to go to the Riviera? Why do you want to walk around a port and look at the boats?"

Now I can see it was an experience of worship for me. I was looking for a ride to riches and romance. Some beautiful woman of untold wealth would invite me on board -- for life! Do you think I could ignore some financial guru who offered me that?

Being free from the need for money changed all that. Now I've got a job to do. If I saw my job was complete -- meaning no more exciting projects to work on -- I might be ready for that yacht. Right now, however, this planet's in tough shape, and with my talents I'm delighted to be one of the guys working to straighten it out. This is a job that turns us on as we emerge from scarcity. The planet can use each of our particular talents.

From the context of sufficiency you will see that the real meaning of your life is seizing the opportunity to make a life-long contribution to others. Donella Meadows, in her eye-opening book *Global Citizen*, suggests that the ultimate purpose of money is the enhancement of human welfare.

When you take on something that requires you to be powerful, you will not be lured by the "something-for-nothing" gurus. Their message is for the limited you -- the one who could never get enough, not the one who is sufficient. In fact, you appear to the gurus as the solution to *their* scarcity. It's not wrong that they want your money for their needs. It's appropriate to the scarcity paradigm. The people who listen to them are unaware that they can operate with sufficiency. The people listening to them are like you used to be, not thinking for themselves. Do you still have a seat in that audience? If so, get up out of it; don't even wait for the intermission. Get a refund if you can. If you can't, not to worry. Consider it an investment in your new future.

Notice who your heroes are. Are they unstoppable with money? Do they use money powerfully or are they trying to accumulate it? Are they selling out or speaking up at their places of work? Are they still working at that "job that sucks" because at least it pays well, or are they coming home every night energized by a work environment of integrity and service?

Is your boss popping pills to get through the day? Are your fellow employees soft and fat? Are you? Do people drink a little too much? Is "T.G.I.F." said more in earnest than in jest? How about absenteeism? And the water cooler bitching and back-biting?

You can change your environment, no matter how hopeless it seems, by taking a stand that you are a person who uses money to serve all people. You may not be popular if you do this, especially with the complainers in your life. Those who are always trying to get something for nothing won't want to hang around you once they see that you're serious about your new way of relating to money.

If your environment still isn't responding, change it. If it's using all your energy, you're constantly getting weaker because you're doing all the work. Get a new group of people around you that are open. Have the rest of your life be about hanging with people who have their attention on serving others. This will ensure that you'll have an extraordinary life.

WHAT YOU HAVE TO LOOK FORWARD TO IF YOU MAKE ENOUGH MONEY

Maybe you've finally made it -- you've got money. Guess who's waiting for you? People who are about to "make it" off your success, that's who -- the advisors, accountants, lawyers, stockbrokers, investment people, business agents, insurance brokers, financial planners, trust officers, bankers, and others who make their living advising those who have made it.

These are human beings who have the same basic addiction you have; they worship money too -- in this case, yours. They have incredible skills and talents. And they are driven by the need for money, even though they look like they have it all together. They've sold their souls over and over again for money. They're in the same domain of scarcity as you and I but with more information about money: "In the land of the blind (scarcity), the one-eyed (money-wise) man is king." They may know more than you or I do about money, but it is within a closed loop, the pinched realm of scarcity where survival rules.

Advisors to the rich are part of the existing paradigm. They're attached to money also. That's why many who have made it have lost it through bad investments, through embezzlement, through legal battles.

Here's what Andrew Tobias says about this in his book *The Only Other Investment Guide You'll Ever Need*:

> "The folks who do understand money, while many have your best interests at heart, have their own interests at heart, too. You've got to stick to sensible investments recommended by competent, disinterested parties. Not competent *or* disinterested, competent *and* disinterested."

I say that people in our culture are never disinterested. It may look that way in the case of some "trustworthy" advisors, but these advisors chase money just as much as anybody else. Why would they devote their lives to helping the rich get richer? Why not build houses, farm, or teach, which might be inherently more fulfilling? Why spend all your time reading quarterly reports, "Barron's," the daily stock market quotes.

Insurance agents who sell to the upper market get their pound of flesh. People worth millions in assets buy huge life insurance policies to protect their estates from inheritance taxes. Often wealthy people are persuaded to pay their life insurance policies in advance. Nothing illegal about this system, but pay attention. A friend of mine sold such a policy and he was bragging about it to me. I asked him how he structured the premiums. He said, the client would pay $50,000 yearly for seven years. I asked him how he structured the commissions. He said, "I took full compensation," (meaning the agent gets paid a percentage on every premium dollar paid in). Perfectly legal.

He told me a third party advisor to the client had asked him to write the policy. So he really hadn't spent much time, nor incurred much in the way of expense. He made a sizable commission for doing very little. I asked him if he had considered structuring the policy so that only part of the premium would generate commissions thereby lowering the cost substantially.

The agent thought I was nuts. "Why would I want to do that?" I pointed out that perhaps some day the client or the advisor would find out that the agent had a choice in designing the policy and that he opted for the big bucks. By being greedy he may have shut off a good source of future business instead of attracting more referrals from an appreciative advisor and/or client. "Mind your own business!" he said, and changed the subject.

I sat at my computer and ran two side-by-side illustrations from the same insurance company. From what the agent told me about the client's age and the yearly premium, if the agent had taken compensation on, say, $10,000 of the premium, the client could have been paying -- for seven years -- an annual premium of $36,000 instead of $50,000. This would have meant that a substantial sum could have gone into the policy annually with no load. According to this calculation, the client was overpaying by close to 40%.

I have no problem with taking the maximum commission if I've produced incredible value for the client or if I've put an enormous amount of time and expense analyzing and meeting with the client. However, I think it is foolish to take the maximum commission for just standing there and selling a product anybody could sell with no value added.

We are all like magnets, in that we attract certain types of people. The people around us are correlated to us, our attitudes, and beliefs. We aren't victims. The so-called victimizers are drawn to us. They have no more choice than iron filings attracted to a magnet. I pointed this out to a millionaire who was complaining to me about an insurance agent who he felt had ripped him off. After talking with me about this incident for some time he began to see it differently. He said, "Oh no. You mean it's not bad luck that has me fleeced by people, it's how I'm being that attracts types like him?" Exactly! He saw that the self-serving agent was attracted to him, and to people like him.

Such self-serving agents will just go away when you take a stand that you are sufficient. When your attention is not on acquiring, hoarding, getting every bargain and possessing, you won't be attracted to deals that formerly hooked you.

TAKE YOUR STAND, THEN MAKE IT REAL

Once you've created yourself as a person no longer run by money, you need to share your liberation. Work it into every conversation. Ask others to support you. Speak in a way that opens the possibility of emancipation from money for everyone with whom you interact.

As a financial advisor with hundreds of clients, I am in a good position to share my insights with clients, both through the review meetings I hold with them and through written communication. I know I have something to say that will make a difference. Many of my clients encourage me to keep writing them about money. In the past I did this mainly through our newsletter, "The Traband Times."

However, at best only a few thousand people would hear me even if my clients pass my newsletter on to others. This doesn't compare to the possibility created by this book, the possibility for millions of people to get free from the bonds of money, from the structure of scarcity. Let me repeat myself.

Speak your stand into existence and it will become real. Talk about it, promote it, brag about it, the more you share it, the more people will begin to relate to you as the person you're becoming instead of the person you've been. As you let them know that you are limitless, resourceful, and sufficient, they'll treat you that way. "We teach people how to treat us," is how best selling author Wayne Dyer puts it. If they treat us as if we're weak, it's because we taught them to do that.

I'm aware that this talk about taking a stand and making it real is new, and that it can be mistakenly assimilated into the current paradigm, a paradigm which makes no distinction between a "stand" and a "resolution." In order to make this distinction totally clear, I will address it from a number of perspectives.

Resolutions exist in the realm of doing. A resolution is characterized by righteousness -- it's the "right" thing to do; by obligation one should promise to do or not do something; by rigidity -- "always" or "never"; and by sacrifice -- having to give up some pleasure (like smoking or drinking) in order to do the right thing. When one lives by resolutions, one is "resolute": "having or showing a fixed, firm purpose". The key word here is "fixed."

By contrast, stands exist in the realm of being or creation. They are characterized by freedom and flexibility. The moment we take a stand, we feel powerfully freed up from "the shoulds." We become new people. Whatever we are now standing for becomes ours, not something imposed by society. We are saying who we "be" -- who we *are* in the matter.

For example, when we marry, we take a stand for the lifelong well being of another person. In taking a stand for friendship we are saying, "I am your friend. You are safe with me. Nothing you do can screw it up." It is not conditional. In taking a stand for power and control over money I am saying, "Who I am in the matter is a person who uses money to serve all people."

Another characteristic of stands is that they are invented. You won't get very far if you just parrot my words and examples. This is thinking you will need to do by and for yourself. You may want to start with the question: "Who can I count on myself to be from now on about money and possessions, regardless of my circumstances?" This is your chance to get out in front of the train of conformity and lay new track. You will need to be bold, will need to act out of your commitments instead of your considerations.

When I really got serious about this project to create a new paradigm for money in the world, I saw that it would take far more than writing a book, hosting a TV show, becoming a public speaker. It would take a complete shift in my everyday practices and way of being. I would have to invent myself newly.

BEING USED BY THE NEW PARADIGM FOR MONEY

The more you take this on the more it will take you over. When you bring something powerful into existence, and start speaking it everywhere, it takes on a life of its own and begins to use you. Simply saying that you're freed up with money can alter your life. The old gripes will be inappropriate, out of tune. You will no longer be attracted to complaining. Sports won't seem as significant. It won't matter so much who wins -- you'll be able to enjoy every game regardless of the outcome.

You'll get annoyed when people feel sorry for you and relate to you as the bundle of complaints you've been. You'll become a robust money mover, a person in action. People close to you won't recognize you when you first become powerful with money. At the same high school reunion in 1990 where I surprised the "girls" with my dancing, an old friend greeted me with, "Hello, Big Money." Standing right next to me was another classmate worth millions. The old friend didn't know much about either of our circumstances, but he'd read about the fulfillment of our $100,000 pledge to The Hunger Project. I was showing up as "Mr. Money" for him.

That year I was inviting people in The Hunger Project to join the Charter Group, which means contributing at least $100,000 in one year. I was presenting the opportunity to approximately 400 Hunger Project volunteers and staff, from age 13 up to senior citizens. I shared about the ridiculous fun my wife and many of the other Charter Group members were having. I asked if anybody in the room would *like* to be in the Charter

Group and have the fun I was having. Most of the people raised their hands.

Then I asked people to raise their hands if they *intended* to get themselves into the Charter Group within ten years, only 50-60 people raised their hands. Those who didn't, began to realize that they had just acknowledged the limits they had imposed on their futures. There was nervous laughter.

There are no limits. At the next break, I asked one of the high school students if he intended to give $100,000 in one year within the next 10 years. "Absolutely!" he replied. "By the year 1994!" This kid trusted himself.

Shift the way you perceive money and you will have unintentionally created new distinctions. Once you do this you'll know that you can handle any addiction, and so can anyone else. You get to control your own life.

THE UNTHINKABLE STARTS HAPPENING

Taking a stand is the beginning of a paradigm shift. When a paradigm really shifts amazing things happen overnight. A much-told story is the one about the four-minute mile record being broken by Roger Bannister in 1954. For years prior to his breaking the four-minute "barrier," many people came close to running the mile in four minutes. Within a year of his run, about 200 other people ran the mile in less than four minutes.

These breakthroughs are unpredictable. Within an existing paradigm, the prevailing beliefs do not allow for certain things to happen. And yet, one person reaches down and does what has never been done and the floodgates open. When there is a breakthrough, there is simultaneously a breaking up of the current reality or paradigm. This new money paradigm is being crafted intentionally, by design. There is a small unstoppable group working to cause a breakthrough for humanity.

SOME BENEFITS OF BEING A NEW MONEY PARADIGM PIONEER

When you bring a new *speaking* to old issues, you'll find people paying attention to you. You won't be put off by, "This is the way we do it around here. That's impossible, you're wasting your time."

You could say that we view the world through a filter and that the creation of a new paradigm gives us a new filter. Over the past few years many people have remarked to me that they don't have my reality around money. They're right. Most people do not see the things I see when it comes to money. I see things as possible that most others would never attempt. The life I've been living for more than 15 years has given me, and many of my friends a remarkable and refreshing freedom.

There are already thousands of people who have begun work on creating their own sufficiency. As this number grows we can expect to approach a critical mass -- a moment when a rollover will occur. At that time, sufficiency will be the context for all life. The work you do to invent your own sufficiency is part of this global cultural shift. Every time another person declares himself whole, complete, and sufficient, this declaration makes the world a safer place for all people.

Will you join me on the journey from the familiar yet unknown, into the unfamiliar yet known? Does this sound backwards? Shouldn't I be saying that the familiar is known and the unfamiliar is unknown? What I mean is that whenever we play safe or try to maintain the status quo, we convince ourselves that we "know" what's familiar to us, like we know the sun will rise tomorrow. We really don't know that, but by living our lives as if some basic events are predictable, we feel more secure. Perhaps what we call familiar is actually part of the great unknown. When you write a new rulebook by creating a new paradigm, you are open to the unfamiliar and it becomes what you know. The fear of the unknown disappears when we embrace the mystery of life. Maybe we can really talk to the animals or walk on water, but it's not possible from the existing paradigm.

> Again and again someone in the crowd wakes up,
> He has no ground in the crowd,
> And he emerges according to much broader laws.
> He carries strange customs with him
> And demands room for bold gestures.
> The future speaks ruthlessness through him.
>   - Rainer Maria Rilke

CHAPTER 10

STEP THREE: ACTIONS TAKEN FROM A STAND

"To believe what has not occurred in history will not occur at all, is to argue disbelief in the dignity of man."
- Mahatma Gandhi

TAKING ACTIONS THAT MAKE ONE'S STAND REAL.

In his book, *The Sky's the Limit*, Wayne Dyer asks the question, "What would you do if there were no such thing as money?" He points out that if you work at the things that bring you pleasure, money will chase after you. He says if you are not willing to depart from the norm, the norm of working primarily to get money, you are actually being dishonest, dishonest with yourself.

After reading *The Sky's the Limit*, I had several meetings with my employees in which I encouraged them to follow Dyer's suggestion and pursue their dreams. I told them that if there was anything they would rather be doing than working in an insurance office, I'd support them.

One secretary said she would love to be working with geriatric patients -- she loved older people. She spoke with such passion about this that we all had tears in our eyes. Her obstacle was that she had never been trained for such work. We said we would support her. I told her she could continue to work for me for as long as she needed while she made the transition to working with geriatric patients. We agreed on a period of eight weeks and after that time she would go off to make the kind of difference in the world that would bring meaning to her life.

My main support person and closest friend in the business said that he and his wife would love to live in ski country and manage an inn. Shortly thereafter, his wife took a year off from her job to attend The Restaurant School in Philadelphia to learn the skills needed to manage an inn. Upon completion of her course, the two of them sold their house and moved to California where they invested all their savings in a high-risk, high-tech business in Silicon Valley. She did manage several restaurants during this time. They've since sold that business for a lot of money and are living the dream life near Lake Tahoe.

I miss my friend. He always operated with integrity in our business. He kept me straight. Now we live on opposite coasts and talk on the phone occasionally, mostly about business and sports. I'm happy for him and his wife.

Because we invest the amount of money we do in the Hunger Project, people think Lee and I have a lot of money. To the contrary, we do not have a lot of money. We have no savings and our life insurance policies have maximum loans. Those who have known us for a number of years could not have predicted that we would be able to contribute a total of $600,000 since 1978 to The Hunger Project. Our tax attorney is not comfortable about the amount of debt we have. Yet we give the money and grow more powerful every day. We demonstrate sufficiency as well as talk about it. We shop at thrift shops and have one car. We're ordinary people living on an ordinary street. People are inspired by our power with money, not by our possession of it.

Because we fund the Hunger Project at such a high level, some people consider us generous. We've never been satisfied with "generous" as a characterization of our behavior. We're doing something anyone can do -- that is, promise something you don't see a way to deliver and then use the seemingly impossible promise to make yourself into the person that creates a way to deliver.

We do this for ourselves as much as we do it for The Hunger Project. We, Les and Lee, as we exist the moment before we announce any new promise, cannot possibly pull it off; we're just not resourceful enough. We know we're going to have to reinvent ourselves to be able to deliver on our word. We like that! We mold ourselves into exciting, powerful, and creative people. It's like venturing into unknown territory, where "there be dragons," yes -- but where there is excitement and fulfillment as well.

Over and over we "sourcefully" reinvent ourselves. What we couldn't handle yesterday gets ground up in the new games we create. Our addictions, our character faults, our complaints and frustrations, all these impediments become the stepping stones into the new world of opportunity.

We choose to traffic in an enterprise most people stay away from -- giving money away that we don't have. If we are reluctant to promise big sums of money, what are we really saying about ourselves? Something like this: "I don't think I'm able to create from nothing."

Sure, when I consider the task ahead of me, I sometimes feel overwhelmed. I'll wonder why I ever opened my big mouth. I'll worry that I'm just a big talker and that now my level of incompetence, as in the Peter Principle, will be found out.

But then I'll remember that the reason I did open my mouth was to break through that level of incompetence. When I'm stopped by something -- by some illusion, by some myth, I need to take on something big enough to expose this myth. The bigger the projects I'm working on, the bigger my thinking has to become to handle them.

The area of "money management" this book is cultivating is not very crowded. Damn near everyone is working on ways to acquire money; hardly anyone is working on ways to give it away. There aren't other books like this to read -- no competition!

Have you ever sat in bumper-to-bumper traffic and watched cars whizzing by in the other direction? For whatever reason -- commuting hour, football game, summer seashore traffic -- most people are going where you're going, and it's taking forever. The guys going the other way are going fast as lightning because almost no one is going that way. I can go at top speed in the realm of freedom from money because that thoroughfare is virtually untraveled.

Most conversations I have are pure inventions. And they are show-stoppers. When I start talking about giving away large sums of money, all the other stuff of conversation -- Caribbean vacations, the new high-budget movie, last night's restaurant -- is eclipsed. This is mind-boggling stuff, particularly because Lee and I can be light and innocent about it, "can be" because we are.

HAVE THE PAST BE OKAY WITH YOU

It's virtually impossible to move on to anything powerfully without acknowledging your past. Your past is what got you to your present. In some areas of your life you have probably been a jerk. In other areas you have probably been untrustworthy. Don't try to step over this.

If you've broken your word with someone, set it straight. If you've been getting away with something, knock it off. And if your attitude towards money has been cautious, welcome to the club. Most of us are very cautious about money. Run down the street shouting "I want your money!" and people will run inside and lock their doors.

We need to quit acting like we've got it all together. Being able to tell the truth gives us power. Lying about something is a protective reaction, and it diffuses our power. Telling the truth actually releases our power -- makes it possible for us to generate something big.

Noticing our environment and saying the way it is would be like a fish noticing the water in which it swims, the bird noticing the air in which it flies. Not until we notice and tell the truth about the way things are does it become possible to move to the next level -- possible for the fish to come out of the water and walk upon land, possible for humans to come out of scarcity and enjoy sufficiency.

You might want to acknowledge that you've been busting your butt so you can go live on a boat and tell the world to leave you alone. Tell the truth and you'll have a solid foundation to stand on.

WHAT SHOULD SOMEBODY PAY YOU?

People often complain to me that they're not making enough money. Perhaps they're making $30,000, $50,000 or $100,000. I ask them if they would like to make twice as much money without leaving their company, and they look at me as if I were crazy. "No way," they'll protest, "you don't know my boss!"

"Yes I do, he's probably like most other bosses," I reply. "Not this company," they'll answer. "They only give raises of 5-10%. Nobody doubles her income around here overnight."

In my experience, if you can find out what a company needs and then supply it, the company will pay you handsomely. I tell people to go to their boss and ask what needs to get produced, the production of which would result in a doubling of the department's net income.

They reply, "My boss will think I'm crazy!" That may be true but only because no one has ever asked your boss that question. Give your boss a few days to think about that question and you may well get an assignment that will truly challenge you. And then, mark my words, you'll get to be really creative.

I'm an employer. If an employee comes to me and says he/she is willing to do whatever it takes, consistent with serving our clients with integrity, that would result in *my* personal income doubling this next year, what do you think I would pay for that? Whatever they asked, that's what.

Think about it. After the dust settles, I'm left with *double my income* and *my business is forwarded*. There are no compromises and there are no standards lowered. So what if the employee is now making five times what I'm making? One client-employer told me, "I would have a hard time with an employee making a lot more than I do. After all, it's my company."

"Maybe that's what keeps you from having a breakthrough," I told him. "You've got it set up so that effective people won't be able to get appropriately compensated around you." Because of this discussion, he saw that his ego had been in the way of attracting exceptional people and producing unprecedented results.

Are you profitable? If you work for someone else, perhaps some large employer, do you make money for them? How do you know? Do they agree? If you are profitable, when did that start? How could you measure it? If you're not yet profitable, when do you project being profitable to the business?

Most people have no way of knowing if they are making money for the company. Most people don't even think that's their job. Talk to the person you work for. If you can show that you are profitable, you can justify a raise. Years ago, the great baseball player, Pete Rose, was traded to the Philadelphia Phillies. He asked the Phillies to pay him a lot more money than he had been making and he pointed out to the owners of the team that they would make big profits as a result of signing him. He was right. Within weeks, advanced tickets sales for the upcoming season leaped off the chart. He knew and could prove that he was profitable. Are you?

I tell prospective clients that they will have breakthroughs with their money if they let me handle their insurance. Many of my clients will attest to this. Talk about value-added, the policies I offer cost the same as those of other companies and my customers begin to earn $10,000 to $25,000 more per year out of dealing with me. That's the reality I have created around me.

Get profitable, and let your employer know it.

BECOME A PHILANTHROPIST -- NO EXPERIENCE NECESSARY

My friend Michael doesn't stand out in a crowd. At age 42, he lived at home with his mom. "Give me $200 a week," he would say. "That's all I need."

One day at a Hunger Project meeting, Michael opened up the possibility for himself that *he* is the key to having hunger end by the turn of the century. Without being asked by any of us fund raisers, he began to pledge higher and higher amounts of money to The Hunger Project. And he paid on time. In 1989 he gave $6,000. In 1990, he invited his family to join him in his pledge. Together they gave $80,000.

If you ever raise money for any project or charity, think of the Michaels around you, ordinary people capable of delivering extraordinary sums of money. Has it damaged Michael? To the contrary, you can't get him to shut up. Often we're both on telephone conference calls or in meetings with people who are investing $100,000 or more yearly to The Hunger Project -- millionaires, captains of industry, high-income doctors, Hollywood stars. In this company Michael speaks up; he has something to say, and everybody listens. He's a hero, an "ordinary person" who took a stand and said, "I can't be stopped."

THE MISSING FOUNDATION

Here's the formula that works. Lay your foundation, then build your structure. When speaking with people about their financial planning, hardly anyone wants to talk about having the foundation of an optimal disability insurance plan. "Let's talk about mutual funds, real estate, tax shelters," they'll say -- all those sophisticated structures for increasing wealth. In my opinion the financial community has missed the boat on designing a fail-proof financial plan.

If you tell most financial planners or insurance agents that you want more life insurance, they'll sell it to you. Tell them you want a retirement plan, they'll get it for you. "Save money for college?" Coming right up. Does anyone ask you if you'll be able to "get by" if you aren't able to produce income? Maybe a few advisors. But if you tell them you *don't* want disability insurance, they'll go right on selling you the other stuff, no questions asked.

I say a trustworthy financial advisor's first commitment should be to his clients' viability and individual responsibility. That's the foundation for financial planning. And if you push financial need to its limit you will see that nothing is more important than reliable disability insurance. Everything you think is important can wait or be dealt with in another way -- except your ability to work.

If a financial plan has been built on a foundation of airtight disability insurance, it's not likely to fail. Without a disability insurance policy that will pay you what you will need per month, including increases for inflation, for as long as you will need it, without regard to what disabled you -- you cannot be in control of your future. If the bus hits you or you lose your mind, where will the money come from if you live for another 40 to 50 years?

99

Push another issue to its limits and see how important it is. Suppose you have three young children and you want them to go to college. You want to start a savings program which will fund their education. But what if you put it off for a few years? You'll simply have fewer years to save, requiring a higher outlay per year when you get down to it.

But what if you haven't saved anything and now your oldest is graduating from high school? You could take a second job. You could reduce other living expenses. The kids could pay some or all of the costs. After all, many kids have paid their own way through college. Are you saying your kids are not as resourceful as other people's kids?

If you didn't save money before they were ready for college, if you can't reduce living expenses, if you can't get a second job, if your kids can't or won't work -- there are still at least three other possibilities: 1) borrow the money (and either you or the kids pay it back after college); 2) ask somebody else to pay some or all of the costs; or, 3) tell your kids you can't pay for college.

Their world won't end if you fail to save enough money for college prior to your oldest turning eighteen. On the other hand, if you are unable to hold a job due to a disability and have no alternate source of income, you become dependent -- on somebody or some system.

THE FAST TRACK TO FREEDOM

Let me say it again -- take on a project so big that you will have to have a breakthrough in your thinking about money. Start something that has never been done.

A few years ago, an eleven-year-old boy named Trevor Farrell began bringing food to the homeless on the streets of Philadelphia. His parents drove him in the family van from their comfortable home in the suburbs to a number of steam vents in the city which street people call home. He distributed sandwiches, coffee, and blankets to them, and he did so on a regular basis. In the process of getting to know them, he formed an appreciation of street people, not as "poor unfortunates," but as people with backgrounds, hopes, feelings, commitments, and capacities not unlike those of his own family.

From a one-man effort, Trevor's Campaign has mushroomed into a large and very effective organization. It is staffed by some of the formerly homeless and it feeds thousands. His commitment has drawn national attention to this complex problem. There were people feeding the homeless long before Trevor, but the way in which he went about his work, out of his stand for the possibility that all human beings have dignity and make a difference, has transformed the way we "do charity." What he brought into existence is a partnership between those we have been calling the hungry and homeless, the "have-nots", and those we have been calling the people who have made it, the "haves," in such a way that those labels are fast losing their currency.

There's plenty to be done. For example, if your church raised $200,000 last year for its projects, you can organize a team that will raise $400,000 this year. You can make a personal pledge that scares you into action. If you gave $2000 last year, promise to give (from your own resources and abilities) $10,000 or $20,000 this year.

A few years ago, a man from New York City called me because he'd heard I was an effective fundraiser. He had committed to a project that would take $40,000 a year to be adequately funded and he was having a tough time raising this. I told him either to ask one person for the whole $40,000 or to ask four people for $10,000 each. After we talked for awhile, mostly about my Hunger Project fundraising experiences, he realized that his goal was too small. He was a different man when he got off the phone. His project had grown in just a few minutes.

Get a little wild with your project. Have it go out of control. For example, I was never a good dancer in the conventional sense. I never learned the steps and up until twenty years ago I was too intimidated to do my own thing. Now I let the music take me over and I go nuts on the dance floor. At my 35th high school reunion one of the "girls" I grew up with exclaimed to my wife, "He was never a dancer. What happened? Did he take lessons?" It was no longer the always-in-control Lester who was dancing. Now the music danced me. I had become the dance.

Since I've discovered that operating out of my stands -- and making big promises consistent with my stands -- empowers me, I've extended this way of operating to all areas of my life. In 1990, I took on raising $1,000,000 for The Hunger Project from individuals in the Greater Philadelphia area. Up until this time the largest amount of money received by The Hunger Project from this community in any one year had been $300,000. A million dollars from a community of this size was unheard of. Within a few weeks of making this commitment and sharing it, many powerful people in the community had joined my team. Why? I say because the project was challenging enough to attract boldness and daring. We ended the year with $611,000 in cash, short of the target yet double our record. The leaders of The Hunger Project were asked us how we did it so they could replicate it in other communities. Other cities took on similar projects resulting in a substantial increase in Hunger Project income.

In June of 1981, I attended a Hunger Project meeting led by Lynne Twist, a truly exceptional fundraiser. This was the first year that Lee and I were pledging more than $10,000, and we were thrilled to be able to do it. At one point in the meeting Lynne passed out pledge forms. I looked at the form and put it on the floor under my chair. After all, Lynne wasn't talking to me. Lee and I had already pledged. We were already in up to our eyeballs.

I heard Lynne say that some of the people in the room already had made pledges for 1981. I thought, "That's good, she knows folks like me are here." She then went on to say she was asking those of us with existing pledges to look newly. I thought, "This is too much; I'm already giving all I can." But what created the possibility of a new future for me was her assertion that only big people can be asked frequently for everything they've got.

BIG PEOPLE? I had never thought of myself that way. I took a stand that I was resourceful and I backed it up by increasing our 1981 pledge to $20,000. Right then and there I began to grow into one of the best fundraisers in The Hunger Project. Lynne asked me for enough money to spring me out of my petty thinking -- and I gave it!

Lynne gave me a great insight by asking me for more money. Now *I* began asking people for a lot of *their* money, and I began asking on a regular basis. And many of them began to give it. I found that what annoyed most people was being treated as though they were small. When I asked people, many of them my best friends and insurance clients, for a lot of money over and over again, they grew into people able, and wonderfully *willing*, to give.

GO FOR IT

Take a risk and get into action. You'll never know what you can handle until you get in over your head. You can be sure that life will be more exciting. Take on challenges that will rid you of your attachments. Set up projects that will demand so much of you that you will have to put in everything you've got. In the process you will notice a shift in your attitude towards possessions. Possessions will no longer be the "be all and end all," but rather, resources you can use to accomplish your goals.

Don't be reasonable. Read and take to heart George Bernard Shaw's words, taken from his *Revolutionist's Handbook*.

"The reasonable man adapts himself to the world; the unreasonable man persists in trying to adapt the world to himself. Therefore all progress depends on the unreasonable man. The man who listens to reason is lost. Reason enslaves all whose minds are not strong enough to master her."

What he says points to something really critical in the line, "The man who listens to reason is lost." I hear Shaw using "to reason" to mean "to prove" -- referring to our need to have irrefutable evidence before taking action. You won't find evidence that a new project will work in advance because it's never been done before!

Most people say, "I'll give it my best shot." I don't expect much from a person who ventures forth beneath that banner.

Better to say, "I AM COMMITTED TO DOING WHATEVER IT TAKES TO FULFILLING MY PROJECT. I WILL LEAVE NO STONE UNTURNED IN FINDING THE RESOURCES." "Your best shot" implies failure, that is, unless you happen to get lucky. Go beyond your anticipated breaking point. That's where your life will start. That's where you'll begin to stand out from the crowd -- not because you'll be better than anyone else, but because you are beginning to grow into the possibility of being fully *you*.

When you take on producing results that you have no business taking on, at least in terms of your history, you give yourself a new future. The world will seem to slow down so you can see what's going on, because *you've* speeded up. When you go faster you can see things that others can't see. It's like getting out in front of life. You have a different perspective.

TRUST IN YOURSELF

Clean up your integrity. Every place you're cheating is a drag on every place you're not cheating. I've found that it's impossible to operate with integrity, with wholeness and completeness, in one area and not in all others. As Gandhi said, "Life is one indivisible whole." It may look like cleaning things up will cost you dearly, in time, in money, maybe even in status, but in the long run -- and probably even in the short run as well -- you will come out ahead.

Merely telling the truth, at least to ourselves, gives us a chance to turn things around. For example, acknowledging that we're not going full out in our jobs and/or our marriages will give us a place to start. Don't try to justify going less than 100% by saying, for example, "Well, my spouse isn't going full out either." That's how we keep others, and ourselves small.

George Bernard Shaw writes: "You cannot believe in honor until you have achieved it. Better keep yourself clean and bright; you are the window through which you must see the world." Notice how Shaw splits us in two to keep us whole, into the perceiver and the medium through which we perceive. *You* are both the one looking through the window and the window itself. If your window is dirty you cannot get a very clear view. It's like looking at the world "through a glass darkly." And that's the same way others with dirty windows are looking at us, for they too are looking through windows smudged and splotched with addictions and beliefs.

CREATE MONEY GAMES FOR OTHERS

About fifteen years ago Gordon Starr, a business consultant in San Francisco, announced his intention to raise a million dollars in ten years for The Hunger Project by running marathons, getting others to run with him, and asking others to pledge money. He came up with this great idea of having some contributors put up matching pledges. They would pay only if Gordon and his team raised an equal amount of money. In this way he put pressure on himself to raise the promised amount of money; and he created a game where new contributors could have their contributions doubled. Gordon exceeded his goal. He completed the project in 1990, having raised over $1,500,000.

Around 1984, Gordon started encouraging people to run in the Moscow Marathon with him as a strategic way to raise the million for The Hunger Project and to open the possibility of a partnership in ending hunger between the U.S. and the U.S.S.R. He arranged meetings with top Soviet officials in his quest to bring the leadership of our two countries together to end hunger. In the completion letters he sent every year I began to see the impact Gordon was making on the world. He had made himself into a money magnet; he was making a big difference in the world, while having a lot of fun and giving people a great game to play.

PLANNING FOR RETIREMENT

What is it you want to be finished doing some day? What do you want to retire from? Does what you're doing take something from you rather than giving something to you? If so, get out of it now. Don't tell me that you need to do this job for the money. You can find something that will fulfill you and be useful to others in addition to paying you enough to live the way a fulfilled person would want to live. If you're not presently fulfilled in your work it's *impossible* to make enough money to make up for *that*. Having more money can't fulfill an unfulfilled person. It's like having a tapeworm in your stomach. You can't eat enough to be nourished.

When I was eighteen years old I took the advice of some of my friends and joined the Merchant Marines. I wanted to make good money and the advice was to sail on an oil tanker because the pay was good. Because you're away at sea for a long time you have nothing to spend your money on. What a bummer for a guy who got seasick easily. I threw up nearly every day for a month; my weight went from 125 to 110, and all for money. I left the Merchant Marine after exactly 30 days!

If you could have it all, and I say you can, you would not want to retire. If you were producing great results for people and your main motivation was to serve them, retirement would not look attractive to you. What looks so great about sitting around? Why would anyone look forward to a time when they weren't going to be fully used? What is the point of life if we're not expressing ourselves full out?

Give me a person who loves his work. Bertrand Russell said:

"Skilled work, no matter what kind, is only done well by those who take pleasure in it, quite aside from its utility, either to themselves in earning a living or to the world, through its outcome."

Take your life in your hands. Change the focus of your life from getting money to giving service. You can be manipulated so easily by the desire for money. Choose service. When you do, a new world will open up -- for you and for me, and, in time, for everyone on the planet.

THE COST OF INACTION

There are people reading this book along with you. Some, indeed maybe *you* among them, have already started transforming their lives. Money now looks different to them. Real estate agents and house painters and dentists are inquiring into the distinction of can't-miss investment as a way of presenting the services they offer. Likewise people who sell products -- such as cars, stereos, and wallpaper -- are learning to present their products in a way that has their purchasers relate to them as investments.

And fundraisers are creating their charitable projects as programs that contribute to the investors as well as to those they are investing in. Heads of organizations are setting up meetings with their staffs to alter the focus of their organizations towards true contribution. A new paradigm brings a new way of looking at things, a new way of solving problems.

I say that aliveness -- which comes from being at risk -- is the new wealth. If I have the ability to put all my money at risk, I have everything; because I can create again whatever I lose. In the new paradigm for money, there is no losing, only using.

Most people are suffering about money. It seems to have a life of it's own. How did money get so powerful? Why do we do all these slimy things to get and keep money? It's embarrassing.

In 1985 I lost four of my best clients within a 12-month period. They were all people from my hometown that I had known for twenty or more years. All four had become very successful. They all dropped their insurance with me and bought from different insurance agents. I couldn't figure out why this was happening, but it sure wasn't what I wanted to have happen. I had nurtured these accounts from the days when they weren't so successful and now they were starting to pay off nicely. This was not a good trend.

Around that time I took a powerful course called the Landmark Forum, which can best be described as a guided inquiry designed to have people think for themselves. It's a challenging thing, to really begin to think for one's self. As Rita Mae Brown says in her novel, *Six of One*, "Thinking is so difficult, the majority prefer to judge instead."

In this course it was suggested that each of us was carrying around a fifty-pound weight on our shoulders and that possibly we would be able to identify it by the end of the course. If we could notice it and identify it, we would be able to remove it.

I used the Landmark Forum to inquire into the loss of these good customers. On the fourth day of the Landmark Forum something popped for me that changed my life. I saw that I was being too concerned with how much money I was going to make on the insurance these people bought. My recommendations and my attitude had become more correlated with Lester getting paid than with my clients being provided what they needed at the lowest possible price. No wonder these clients had dropped me. It was surely noticeable on some level that I was "putting a spin" on my recommendations to them. How revealing!

Right then and there I saw how easy life could be if I stopped "putting a spin" on my advice and simply told people everything I knew. I could simply be straight with people and tell them where to find the best deals. If I didn't get his or her business, I'd get someone else's. If I didn't get enough business to live the way I wanted to live, I would get out of the insurance business and into something new.

I was a free man when I walked out of that course. Now I am straight with people and people appreciate that. After every interaction I can look back and see that I have been straight with people. I can put everything in writing or meet any competitor face to face with the client present. The angst has gone out of my business life, and my clients no longer leave me. I pay my taxes on time and with full disclosure. I fill out loan forms completely. If the banks know everything about me they may not want to loan me money or they may charge me higher interest, but whatever happens is built upon the foundation of my integrity. So it cannot crumble.

A few months before I had this breakthrough about money my wife and I were on a five-week trip through Europe. We rented a car and as usual we declined to take the collision damage insurance. Towards the end of the trip I scraped the side of the car on a wall. I went into a supermarket in Italy and bought spray paint and painted over my scratch so I wouldn't have to pay for the repair.

When I turned the car in in Zurich with an attempt at nonchalance, I was hoping the clerk wouldn't notice my artistry. She went out and inspected the car and came back into the office filled with clerks and customers and asked in a loud voice, "Vot haf you done vis de car?" I was mortified. It suddenly got very hot in that office.

I feebly replied, "I scraped it on a wall." Looking me square in the eye she asked, " Yah, but den vot did you do vit de car?" I gestured weakly, "I painted it." All the people in that office were now looking at me. Then she said, "Come wit me." We inspected the car and it looked horrible. I told her to get it fixed and put it on my American Express card. Like I had a choice!

That incident woke me up. Now I let waiters know when they undercharge me. Before this I called it to their attention only when I was overcharged. Now, as a person freed up about money, I make sure I pay the fair price.

PUTTING YOURSELF SOURCEFULLY AT RISK

If you say you are going to use money in the service of others, you are trusting yourself to invent something. You and I have the ability to invent a reality and then live it moment by moment. I find it exciting to be a pioneer in this new money paradigm. It puts me out on the skinny branches of the tree where I can discover how resourceful I am, and how capable of "balancing." I use this to produce a state change in myself, something that will blow my mind.

If you are passionate about something -- like building a new library for your community or having your neighborhood free of drugs -- promise to contribute a lot of money to the effort. Here's what I mean by a lot. If when I say $5,000, you think I'm talking to someone else, promise $5,000 spread over the next 12 months. Maybe your number is $25,000 or higher. Have it be a number that breaks you out of your present reality of contribution, a number that gives you a new and exciting future.

I speak regularly with heads of charitable organizations and other people responsible for fundraising. When they hear that The Hunger Project has many donors who contribute $5,000, $25,000, or $100,000 a year, they assume that we must have a lot of wealthy people supporting us. In their reality, people of modest means do not give that much money away.

But many of the people who give $5,000 a year have annual incomes of $50,000 or less. It's not uncommon for people who didn't earn much more than $100,000 the prior year to pledge that amount. And most of them find a way to deliver. They, like I, commit to earning additional money to give to The Hunger Project.

The Hunger Project sees people as resourceful, not limited by their history. Our experience has been that people have simply been waiting for a big enough game to draw them out.

Most organizations treat their contributors with kid gloves; they encourage them to give a reasonable amount. That's insulting.

When you ask people for an *unreasonable* amount, you are acknowledging them as capable of coming up with it. People who are considering giving a lot of money soon get in touch with their ability to create. They lighten up, and money starts to get freed up for them. So they give some more -- and lighten up still more!

HOW GAMBLING KEEPS US STUCK IN THE OLD PARADIGM

We have legalized gambling in our country. In New Jersey, there's Atlantic City, and out west there's Las Vegas and Reno. And you can buy lottery tickets on every street corner. There are horse and dog racing tracks everywhere. Millions of people bet on football, basketball, and baseball games. Then there are the card games and the bingo games. This is an enormous industry.

When I was a serviceman in the Air Force back in the fifties, I learned how to gamble. My teacher went on to become one of the best poker players in Washington, D.C., after he left the military. He made his money on other people's addiction to gambling. In the Air Force, my buddy taught me how to get the odds on my side before I entered any game of chance. If you can arrange the odds in your favor, he said, you don't need luck. If you can't get the odds on your side, you'll need an unusual amount of luck just to break even.

We played blackjack at the Base Casino. As you know, the odds in blackjack are on the side of the dealer. When a player hit blackjack, he became the new dealer. But most of the guys were reluctant to be dealer, so when they hit blackjack my friend and I bought from them their right to deal. We made money from this every payday. The casinos make money from this 24 hours a day. It ain't gambling. It's a sure thing. The casinos have a sure thing. It's a business for them just like selling washing machines. One way to get the upper hand on money is to stop gambling.

And I mean stop gambling even if you have the odds on your side. It's demeaning to the people you fleece and it doesn't say much for you. I say the real juice in life comes from being of service to others, not preying on their addictions. Be straight with people. Stop taking their money and you'll heal yourself in the process.

Chain letters are another example of being powerless with money. If you think, you'll realize that even if the chain isn't broken somewhere down the line the money is going to run out. If each person enrolls at least two other people to keep the chain moving ultimately all the people on the planet will be in the chain, and there will be nobody left to enroll.

PICK UP THE CHECK

If you go out to dinner with other people and it's not clear who's paying, either say you're buying or agree to split the check. It's a great feeling -- and a powerful statement of sufficiency -- to simply pick up the tab, "for no reason."

I used to be a guy who "headed for the men's room" -- sometimes literally -- when the check was on its way to the table. Now I always have enough money to pick up every check and I'm willing to pay all the time. As a result, I've never been treated so much in my life.

In August of 1989 my wife and I were introduced to Vanessa Redgrave backstage in London following her performance in Martin Sherman's "A Madhouse in Goa." Martin is my wife's cousin. A few months later we invited Vanessa to dinner in New York, where she was performing in another play, so that we could introduce her to the late actor Raul Julia and his wife Merel, who had become friends of ours through the Hunger Project.

I figured it was my treat and I knew that it could cost as much as $1,000, especially if we drank a few bottles of good wine.

I did order great wine as an accompaniment for an outstanding dinner in a fine restaurant. I was ready when the check came but Raul insisted on paying it. I saw that he would be insulted if I paid. So we had a great night with great people and I had an extra $1,000 that could now be re-allocated.

People who are free from money don't duck the check. They pick it up with pleasure. You'll enjoy your meal much more if you get into this habit. Indeed you'll feel like a millionaire; and others -- mark my words -- will follow your example. This one simple action will benefit you as much if not more than it will benefit others.

Don't be petty. *Always* pay your share, or more. Don't hassle over the check, adding and dividing it up and being a jerk in public. Pay it -- discreetly, not boastfully -- and reap the rewards in a thoroughly enjoyable and companionable meal. Also, tip more than the customary 15%. That will include the wait staff in the generous and genial spirit of the occasion.

HOW TO ASK FOR WHAT YOU WANT

Do people get upset with you when you ask them for something? Is asking unpleasant for you? Do you have to tiptoe around when making requests? Or are you a demander? "Just do what I say. I'm the boss, the father, etc." There is a way to ask people for things that almost always produces a pleasant experience all around and frequently results in your getting exactly what you want -- even helps you *find* out what you want.

It's an art called invitation. You can learn it best by doing the basic course offered by Landmark Education Corporation called the Landmark Forum. Here, you'll learn to ask in such a way that the other person feels authentically acknowledged and appreciated whether they accept or decline your request. They get the feeling that no aspect of your relationship with them will suffer as a result of their response, even though it's obvious that you have a preference in the matter.

The other recommendation regarding requests is to ask people for a lot. People can handle a lot more than we normally ask of them. Perhaps the discomfort around asking is that we ask for too little from people, and on top of that we're tentative. No wonder people get upset. Ask for everything you think they've got and then some and convey to them that you'll be satisfied with whatever they give. They can handle it -- and they'll love you for seeing them as limitless.

Trust yourself to swing out. If you make a big money commitment, you'll now have to be an entirely different person to fulfill it. You'll need to rearrange your molecules. The way in which you produced results before will not be sufficient to deliver this one. So you get to invent yourself as equal to the new task. You have generated having yourself be at risk, which you will find also generates being resourceful. And as you become more and more resourceful you will find yourself an ever more powerful *generator* of resources, resources of every kind -- including, of course, money.

CHAPTER 11

THE KEY TO ONGOING POWER AND CONTROL OVER MONEY

HERE WE GO

The preceding chapters were directed at having you take a stand that you are sufficient. Sufficient means resourceful and able. Once you declare your own sufficiency, the next move is to express yourself from that newly created context. If you've begun operating as a sufficient person, the way to confirm sufficiency as your reality is to tell those around you -- to tell them that you are sufficient, that you are resourceful, that you are able to handle anything.

There is a kind of speaking that is particularly effective in creating this new context of sufficiency. It's called *sharing*. By sharing I mean being intimate, expressing to another your feelings, expressing your love and your vision, allowing your true self to be known.

The opposite of sharing is withholding. All too often we keep our feelings, our caring, and our resources to ourselves. This "hoarding" arises out of our belief in scarcity -- out of our belief that there isn't enough of anything to go around. But whatever we hold on to ultimately acts to suppress us.

In my experience, whenever I withhold, my resources diminish. By contrast, when I share what I have, my resources expand. People hoard not only tangible things, such as money, they also hoard intangible things, such as love. I am not saying that hoarding is bad or wrong. Indeed, it is an appropriate behavior for people whose reality is scarcity -- for people who feel the need to hold on to what they have and accumulate more. By contrast, people whose context is sufficiency feel the need to share what they have.

You cannot create a context of sufficiency subscribing to and engaging in the beliefs, the actions, and the conversations arising out of scarcity. You need to engage in actions and conversations arising out of sufficiency. And the most critical action, the most critical conversation, is that of sharing.

Sharing is *speaking into existence* what you intend to create. It is making something real by declaration. When you begin to experience the joy of sharing, you will see how incomparably more satisfying it is than whatever people experience out of their hoarding. And the more you share the freer you'll get.

When sharing happens people enroll. They enroll in you and in what you're doing. They want what you've got. If you tell them that you're getting something great out of going to church, they'll go to church with you. If you tell them that you got something great from a book, they'll read it. If you share how great your life is since you did a particular seminar, they'll sign up for that seminar.

If they're not enrolling, you're either not sharing or you're not sharing effectively. "Telling about something" is not sharing; "telling about something" is detached and descriptive, the kind of thing a reporter might write. It doesn't give the listener true access. There is no emotion, no vulnerability, nothing at stake. No one is taking a real risk. Almost all of our everyday conversation is "telling about."

Another kind of non-sharing is *sharing in order to*. This is when you want the other person to do something. It's when you have an agenda and you are manipulating another in order to get the result you want. You are directing the conversation "in order to ...." SHARING "IN ORDER TO" IS A SCARCITY BEHAVIOR. It bespeaks one's need for something. It is controlling and manipulative. By contrast, when you are genuinely sharing, you relinquish control, you allow yourself to be open and vulnerable. Only people who are standing for their sufficiency can afford to be vulnerable. All others must protect themselves.

"Sharing in order to" comes out of fault-finding. You want the other person to change, and you know that this idea, this seminar, or this activity will be good for this person. He or she is overweight, lonely, depressed, whatever -- badly in need of some kind of breakthrough; and out of the goodness of your heart you are recommending such-and-such.

Authentic sharing is making your life available to others, not laying it on them. It is going public with your breakthroughs and insights. By bringing new ideas and commitments to their attention, you open up possibilities for them. You are like an explorer reporting back on unknown territory. Your report may not "make sense," given the existing reality, but by sharing it with others you open up the way to a wider, freer, and more empowering understanding.

Earlier in the book I shared with you about making pledges to my church and my son's private school, pledges that I did not fulfill originally, but which I did fulfill later. I fulfilled these pledges to clear my conscience, yes, but even more so I did this to declare my sufficiency. And by sharing this experience with you I further solidify my stand for my sufficiency.

Writing this book has made me more sufficient. As I make myself more vulnerable to you I become more capable. Sharing enables me to outfit myself. It's like equipping myself for a trip, the trip of life. And the more I share, the more I become aware of how much more I have to share.

If you are determined to create a world of sufficiency you must enroll your network in the sufficiency conversation. You may be familiar with the phrase; "There's no honor among thieves." Think about it. Your world is the world of scarcity. You will not readily find sufficiency in this world -- it must be created. You must invent it and share your invention with others. This is the work of enrollment.

The more you share, the richer your life -- and the lives of your family and friends -- will become. As you renounce the significance of those things that formerly "possessed" you, you will be set free. How can you best practice this sharing? Start by telling those around you what you are up to, and how what you are up to has broken money's hold on you. Let them know of any breakthroughs you've already experienced. You could share how your past practices with money were inconsistent with your present stand. In the process of sharing you will notice that the more obvious failures of integrity have been addressed, but that the more subtle ones are still with you.

That's what happened when I began sharing. The sleazy things I was still doing around money revealed themselves; I was shocked to see how convoluted and entrenched my sleaziness was. Fortunately I had a group of supporters and coaches. They were there to remind me of -- and to reinforce -- my commitment to be "clean and straight"; and they helped illuminate those areas where I wasn't, so that I could clean them up. It was a blessing to be so clearly confronted. And it's not only in the area of money. Recently I cut down on my sugar intake, began exercising, became a vegetarian: all at the age of 54.

HERE'S THE KEY! Let other people know that you appreciate them. And particularly acknowledge their generosity. Don't be stingy in acknowledging others or yourself. *Stinginess in any form is correlated to scarcity.* Give people things that are precious to you. Keep building on your stand that you are sufficient. *You* are your main asset, not those figures on your financial statement. You will see your friends showing up as sufficient out of your practice of acknowledging them. You'll find them complaining less, find them handling those things that had them stopped.

The world needs your speaking and your actions. All around you people are shackled by their beliefs about money. They can't move very well. They are crippled and hurting. And often they are in denial about their pain. For example, when African leaders got together in the past, many of them denied that their countries had hunger problems. "No problem," they were saying. "We're doing as well as anybody else."

"Sharing" is not being righteous about something. Sharing is done to promote something that you are creating. By sharing you can open up a new future for other people and support them in realizing that future. The paradigm you are creating comes into existence when you share; it becomes real both for you and for those with whom you share.

SHARE YOUR PRODUCTIVITY -- EMPOWER UPWARDS

One client of mine was managing a company for another client of mine, and during a conversation I had with him about management techniques, I remarked, "It seems to me that your job is to make your boss right." He replied, "No, my job is to make him rich. If he's getting richer I'm getting my job done. If he's not getting richer, I'm not getting my job done."

I was startled by this. "Do you mean," I asked, "that if your boss gets richer he'll pay you more money?"

"Perhaps," he replied. "That's up to him. Whether or not I get a raise, my job is to improve the quality of his life -- on his terms." Well, his boss did indeed get richer while my client managed the company. A lot richer. Not surprising. Wouldn't every employer want this kind of attitude in his/her employees? And the manager got at least as much out of it as his boss. He freed himself from his own needs and thus freed himself to go full out in his work. He has since started his own very successful management consulting business, with the full support of his former employer.

If you commit to having your boss get what he or she wants, you'll get more satisfaction out of your work than you ever dreamed possible. If you're working for someone you don't respect you can: 1) stay there and keep suffering; 2) learn to appreciate him/her so you can play full out; or 3) move on to another job.

BE A STAKEHOLDER IN YOUR PLANET

When you share your sufficiency, a by-product is that others will become more sufficient. The new paradigm for money that I'm standing for hasn't been created. We need partners to create it; we need to share it with others, one by one, until it lives everywhere. You could be the one that turns the tide for your network of family and friends so that they become powerful with money.

When we have created the reality that no one wins unless everyone crosses the finish line together, all actions will align to be consistent with that. If what you're up to is having a world that works for everyone with no one and nothing left out, you'll need to become powerful with money, you'll need to become "unstoppable." When something is critical or necessary, a person who has empowered himself gets the money to make it happen. When we take a stand that something is critical, like saving someone's life or ending hunger, we become the powerful person who finds the money to make it happen. A powerful stand literally calls the money forth.

People who are powerful with money are ordinary human beings with extraordinary commitments. They have taken the stand that they are who they say they are, and they take actions consistent with that stand. This power is available to all of us.

To be a stakeholder in our planet, take a stand for your sufficiency. In sharing that stand, and in taking actions consistent with sufficiency, *your* freedom from scarcity will promote, and in time produce, a like freedom -- in ever-widening and ultimately global circles around you.